A GEOGRAPHY OF

population
and settlement

THE BROWN
FOUNDATIONS OF GEOGRAPHY
SERIES

Consulting Editor
ROBERT H. FUSON
University of South Florida

A GEOGRAPHY OF

Agriculture
James R. Anderson, University of Florida
Transportation and Business Logistics
Edwin J. Becht, University of Oklahoma
Plants and Animals
David J. de Laubenfels, Syracuse University
Geography
Robert H. Fuson, University of South Florida
The Atmosphere
John J. Hidore, Indiana University
Population and Settlement
Maurice E. McGaugh, Central Michigan University
Industrial Location
E. Willard Miller, The Pennsylvania State Universit
Water
Ralph E. Olson, University of Oklahoma
Earth Form
Stuart C. Rothwell, University of South Florida
Minerals
Walter H. Voskuil, University of Nevada

THE BROWN
FOUNDATIONS OF GEOGRAPHY
SERIES

A GEOGRAPHY OF
population
and settlement

HB
1951
M3

MAURICE E. McGAUGH

Central Michigan University

WM. C. BROWN COMPANY PUBLISHERS
DUBUQUE, IOWA

THE BROWN
FOUNDATIONS OF GEOGRAPHY
SERIES

Consulting Editor
ROBERT H. FUSON
University of South Florida

Copyright © 1970 by
Wm. C. Brown Company Publishers

ISBN 0–697–05157–9

Library of Congress Catalog Card Number: 74-118885

Printed in the United States of America.

Geography is one of man's oldest sciences, yet it is as new as the Space Age. Knowledge of the earth obtained from satellite photography and measurement, remote sensing of the environment, and by means of other sophisticated techniques are really but a stage in the evolutionary process that began with ancient man's curiosity about his surroundings. Man has always been interested in the earth and the things on it. Today this interest may be channeled through the discipline of geography, which offers one means of organizing a vast amount of physical and cultural information.

The **Brown Foundations of Geography Series** has been created to facilitate the study of physical, cultural, and methodological geography at the college level. The **Series** is a carefully selected group of titles that covers the wide spectrum of basic geography. While the individual titles are self-contained, collectively they comprise a modern synthesis of major geographical principles. The underlying theme of each book is to foster an awareness of geography as an imaginative, evolving science.

Preface

Two topics named in the title of the book are presented together as the basic theme of the study: human population and settlement. They are treated together from the first to the last of the text. A central idea dominates: Man is at work and in residence in area. The study examines the distributions of population over the earth's surface, and it notes what man is doing and how well he lives. The theme of settlement is presented along with a discussion of the distribution of population itself. The study deals with the pattern of man's use of the land, of the physical installations he has made, of his use of the resource base, and of his communities. It deals with the forms of his livelihood. The structure of the settlement is treated along with the distributions of human numbers.

Economic and social elements of human settlement are analyzed as they relate to man's distributions. Populations differ in density among the world's regions. They differ also in their forms of livelihood and in their well-being. Standards of living, of health, and of literacy differ. Also, there are vast differences in incomes and in economic stature. Man's habitations, the plants in which he finds employment, his transportation and communication networks all are a part of the settlement. It is reasonable and appropriate to approach the theme of geography by having population and settlement combined as one theme.

The author has consulted many books and references on population and on settlement. Censuses and monographs have been studied along with periodicals which have offered analyses of population data and growth rates. Several new books on human geography and on cultural geography have been helpful with the theme of settlement. Special mention must be made of the demographic records of the United Nations. Also, the publications of the Population Reference Bureau have been invaluable. The theme of the geography of settlement came during long discussions with Dr. Henry M. Leppard, Professor Emeritus of the University of Chicago. The writer can only hope that Dr. Leppard approves of this brief treatment of so vast a subject.

Maurice E. McGaugh

Introduction

The earth now has more than three billion human residents. In some regions there are great concentrations of settlement, but in others so few people are present that vast areas seem to be undeveloped frontiers. The unevenness of the distribution is remarkable because there is a full set of underlying reasons for the differences from place to place. Related to the patterns of population are those of people's activities and livelihood. Some reasons are inherent in the cultural, economic, or political bases which have come out of the historic past. Others are evidences of the present stages of technological development of differing groups of neighboring human contemporaries. Accessibility and opportunity for communication among human groups may affect settlement, making it sparse in some areas and very dense in others. In many ways a population map shows evidences of adjustment to sets of physical conditions which have offered critical advantages or disadvantages for human settlement.

Study of human population and its distribution is the core of geography. Without considering people and their activities, there is little meaning in the discipline. Man's distributions and the relationships of these distributions within the physical patterns of the world are the basis for geographic study. Every one of the billions of people has a place for himself. Every one has his own set of activities which he performs. His own livelihood and that of others result in patterned forms of activity. These, in turn, reflect themselves in patterns of settlement.

Every individual is a part of the geographical pattern of human settlement. He is responsible to some degree or other for the total pattern. His own activities are performed within the human and cultural framework of the whole complex. Evidences of his activities may be numerous or few. In the more favored regions the marks of himself and of his neighbors are clearly visible. He may make his contribution in remote regions, too, because he will make excursions into them. He and his companions may even erect settlements in out-of-the-way and inhospitable areas. These may be very important and large or may be very small. The established settlement to which he belongs may maintain such outposts in remote places because of the strategic advantage obtained or because there may be an opportunity to gain a supply of a special resource.

Simply stated, man is at work and in residence in area. The distributions of his settlements and of his occupations and his degree of well-being are far from uniform. The world's population, its major distributions and the patterns of settlement resulting from man's activities are the proper subject matter for geography. This study will be an examination of the distributions of population in area, and it will note what man is doing there. Evidences of man and the features that show his work and which show his residence and distributions constitute the patterns of human settlement.

Contents

WORLD POPULATION DENSITY

INHABITANTS PER SQUARE MILE

| Under 2 PRACTICALLY UNINHABITED | 2 to 25 SPARSE | 25 to 125 MODERATE | 125 to 250 | Over 250 DENSE |

Chapter 1

Elements of Population and Settlement

The Population Map

The map of human population is the most important map of all for a human geographer. This is why the *Frontispiece* of this study is a world map showing the distribution of the world's peoples. A population map is a map of human settlement, too, because the arrangement of man's cultural features matches that of man himself. Immediately one can see on the map the areas which hold heavy concentrations of population. Significantly, one also notes the "empty spaces." Both of those distributions stand in bold outline in their relationships to the continents and within favored regions within the continents. They show as well the parts of the world's land masses which are unfavorable for people. Thousands of people live on each square mile in selected regions, but very few or almost none at all are often found in inhospitable and forbidding areas.

The Settlement Pattern

Geographers are concerned with the phenomena of man-created or man-dominated distributions on the earth's surface. These include man's habitations and communities, the places for his creative work, the patterns which show his use of the land and its resources, the other man-made physical installations, and his lines of transportation and communication. These combined evidences of the human occupation of earth may be termed the settlement pattern. Evidences of man and his occupational structure constitute the visible distributions of geography. The student must study man in his areal distributions and relationships.

Human Settlement and the World's Physical Patterns

There is a correspondence of patterns when the map of human population is studied and is compared with maps which show basic geographic patterns, such as physical maps showing the relief and the basic distributions of the land forms. Climatic maps, vegetation and soils maps, and others show basic distributions which relate to the density of human population. Maps which record distributions of economic resources, as mineral deposits, and those which show the areas of production for a commodity of trade, and others correspond with maps showing distributions of settlement. The location of some settlements shows that access to the sea is important. Other concentrations of settlement show that there are advantages within the continental interiors. Again, still other settlement patterns may be extended along a long line of communication.

A comparison of the world's population map with those of the earth's physical patterns shows some significant relationships. Population concentrations must avoid the areas of the great mountain systems. The great deserts are avoided. So, too, the tropical rain forests hold few people. By a very notable contrast, the areas of the tropical savannas seem to invite dense settlement in some of their regions, but in others they repel settlers. All high latitudes with their cold climates restrict the number and size of settlements. In a very true sense the world's population map combines with a set of physical maps to show positive and negative factors affecting human settlement.

Human settlement concentrates population in regions and areas which offer special opportunities for living and livelihood of large numbers of people. There must be advantages in those locations which are far above those of the world's averages. A prime factor is the incidence of arable land. This is, of course, a generalization for many categories of land. The definition must vary because land may be productive in many ways, depending upon the ways the population group uses it and upon the sustenance which it is made to provide to that population group. Notably, too, the use of land in a given region may be culturally dictated, and so the demands may be very different from those of another population group even though the land resources are similar.

There must be other resources besides that of arable land if the human population is to prosper in a region. Minerals are needed in adequate supply and variety; forests and their products are important; there may be special products derived from animal sources. Even the oceans and other water bodies may contribute to the stock of resources. All these, and more, offer special opportunities for concentrations of settlement. Their availability is reflected often in the distributions of settled areas.

The set of the world's climates relates significantly to the distributions of human settlement. Traditionally, many writers have indicated this as a dominant factor in limiting or encouraging use of the world's regions. It has been proved long ago that climate playing the dominant role as a control of settlement distributions is a wrong conclusion. Nevertheless, it is true that climate is interwoven with other basic elements in the physical landscape. A so-called trinity of *climate, vegetation,* and *soils* has been studied and analyzed as a set of geographical elements which are always to be considered when human occupancy of an area is concerned. However, they do not dictate human settlement or its form.

Climate and its related elements are constantly to be considered as the world's peoples set up and build their settlements. There are many modifications and adjustments and there are evolving changes and transitions while the patterns of settlement evolve in time. An illustration today is that many population groups have the ability to modify their living conditions so they can offset climatic disadvantages, and so they can now use regions which were forbidding to peoples in earlier times.

Climates of the world may be generalized in two types as far as human settlement is concerned. They are either favorable or unfavorable for man's use. The best of them offer unusual advantages to man. Their benefits may override other important shortcomings so they may seem to invite dense populations. By contrast, many other climatic types are restrictive. People cannot enter such regions in numbers without making unusual efforts. It is usually true that residents of the inhospitable region must have some form of subsidy from regions where there is more opportunity. That resident population must establish strong counter measures with a great deal of planned effort to make living conditions hospitable.

Geographical Elements of Settlement

Patterns of human settlement in densely populated areas are often more easily identified with favorable sets of geographical elements than with those in more rigorous physical settings. Relationships of dense settlements in their regions are complex, however, and they may never be explained simply. There are almost always influences of cultural and historical background which must be studied along with those of the natural setting. Present-day distributions may be the continuation of basic patterns which had origins deep in the past. Older political structures leave their marks everywhere. They may often dominate the total landscape, either by encouraging settlement so that it has grown and prospered, or they may have restricted or held back the use of a potentially valuable area. Cultural influences, past and present, are manifest in the patterns of population and its arrangements of today. Also, economic reasons, varying from competitive cost of production to difficulties of access and transportation or to stages of industrial development, may affect the grosser patterns of human distributions and livelihood.

Accessibility is a factor which affects the density and complexity of settlement. Men from densely settled areas encroach gradually on the less hospitable areas. They work to convert sparsely settled land to a part of the ecumene and may encourage and assist an all-over settlement of the new region. Or they may support excursions into the new region, perhaps establishing outposts in remote or inhospitable areas. They may want the resources of the new region. Populated areas are busy in gaining access to the full set of the world's resources. However, within the densely settled regions there are all gradations of intercommunication, from well coordinated to almost undeveloped. This problem within the respective regions, and inter-regionally as well, leaves a strong mark on the visible elements of the world's settlement.

Not everywhere has the period of human settlement lasted the same length of time. The period of human occupancy has been very long within many favored regions, but in others which still offer considerable opportunity there has been a lag until almost the present time. The settlements of Egypt and Mesopotamia date back more than 6000 years. New Zealand, in contrast, has only recently received its population. Antarctica now has a small population, numbered only in the hundreds, supported from the larger settled communities.

In the longer settled portions of the world, the patterns of settlement have been established and the activities of the people have been built into an economic structure, a patterned form of settlement. By contrast, in many of the inhospitable areas the newness of the settlements may be the most striking features. Small communities of people have long been living in unfavorable locations, but the pressure of population growth in the most recent times has encouraged their growth and planted even more new settlements in remote regions.

A fairly recent need of the more densely settled regions has often placed a subsidy on the production of an inhospitable outpost. Mining communities in regions of intense cold are examples, as in northern Canada or in northern Siberia. Mining centers in the high Andes are old by comparison. Both sets of these settlements of restricted population are permanent in their offerings to the more densely settled regions which depend upon their production and which indirectly subsidize them. The population itself is not as stable as the communities.

Another significant set of outpost communities does not show on an ordinary population map. These are whaling vessels or trawlers working far from their home ports. The bases for the fleets are the visible features of the settlement.

World Settlement Patterns of the Future

The world population has numbered more than 3,000,000,000 persons since the mid-1960's. There will be twice that number by the year 2000 A.D., within the lifetime of many people who are now adults. The certain population growth can cause no other than a spiraling demand for the world's stock of resources, foodstuffs and others. The food supply must be doubled and more, for there must be better living standards than at present for people yet to come. Idealistic though it sounds, this is an objective which must be realized before the beginning of the twenty-first century. Transportation and distribution of necessities and other commodities which men need must keep pace. So, too, must the economic, cultural, and other interrelationships of peoples make a progressive growth. These revisions are necessary, for within four decades the average living space of every person on earth will be cut in half. Nor will numbers cease to grow even at that stage!

As the human population continues to grow, there cannot be other than an increasing pressure on the land base. Density of settlement will continue to increase in the present densely populated areas. Sparsely settled areas will certainly get more than their share of the growing settlement. In addition, there unquestionably will be settlements established in territories now considered impossible for human use. Completely new ways must be found for utilizing the presently known stock of the world's resources. Also, new materials and foods must be developed to fill increasing needs. There must be found new ways to bring the elements of human needs and the forms of human livelihood into a planned geographic pattern. Every region must be made to contribute what it can to the whole legacy. There is a utopian need for a concentrated and cooperative effort. Population growth will not cease at any predetermined number nor within a predictable time.

Geography of
World Population

If the student is to understand the patterns of human settlement today, he must understand the beginnings and the locations of man's early settled areas. Some of the patterns of human distributions were made long ago before the beginnings of history. Numbers of the population then were very small. Settled areas of any size were generally in favored low-latitude situations. Fertile river valleys or deltas, coastal locations, and oasis-like sites along natural routeways provided room for the early communities. Only meager settlements were located in the middle or high latitudes during the prehistoric times.

Great numbers of people have been included in the world's population during only a relatively short time. Although the time of man on earth may span most of a million years, his numbers were so small for all but the most recent centuries that there is little comparison with the population of today. It was not until the time of the "European Discoveries" that there were great numbers of people on earth. Since that time, however, the growth rate has accelerated until it caught the attention of scholars who became students of population. During the nineteenth century in Europe several studies were made on the phenomenon of burgeoning population. Thomas Malthus, working in the 1820's and 1830's, was the writer most publicized for the period. More recently, many twentieth-century observers have been viewing with alarm the present-day "population explosion." Everyone must note the problems for the future in having man double his present numbers by the year 2000 A.D. To gain perspective on the present, one needs to review the record of the world's population growth from the past up to the present time.

The Study of World Population

Many of the present generation may be surprised to find that human population during the past was so small in comparison with the figures of today. Many thousands of years went by before the total world population equaled that of a modern medium-sized country. The great civilizations of the past (and truly they were great!) flourished despite having so few people. Their great cities were wonderful, they produced the "seven wonders of the ancient world," they built ports for shipping and trade, and they had elaborate irrigation projects. Achievements in many cultural efforts, in governmental organization, and in providing records of the past are the more remarkable when one makes comparisons with the records of contemporary countries and communities.

Historians, demographers, and others in research have been working hard during recent decades to construct estimates of the world's population during the past. It has been difficult to arrive at trustworthy figures because there certainly were no censuses and rarely have there been well-authenticated records. It is desirable to have the record extending back into the time long ago, to the time preceding writing or even preceding spoken language. One must be content with estimates, finally, but they clarify the mystery of the numbers of man during the past, and they provide a fine fund of information on his distributions.

An important reference to the topic of the world's population of the past has been provided recently by the Population Reference Bureau, of Washington, D. C. A study by Annabelle Desmond and others in 1962 uses several United Nations studies, along with the works of other demographers and historians. A graph prepared for the study, titled *How Many People Have Ever Lived on Earth?*, is reproduced in *Figure 2.1*. The figure entitled "Growth of Human Numbers" presents a record of the world's population totals during more than 500,000 years. It presents the estimates for the Old Stone Age and the New Stone Age as extending forward in time until about 3000 B.C. Population was skimpy indeed during those long periods preceding the ages of metals. Some important acceleration in population growth came during the early historic periods, recorded as beginning about 3000 B.C. These were the times of achievement when the ancient world came into its own.

The basic point of the Population Reference Bureau study is to show how population has been growing at an accelerated rate since the earliest beginnings of the human race. Also, it anticipates future growth, making predictions in the context of analyses of the United Nations research teams, forecasting the growth trend until the year 2000 A.D. The summation of the figure's meaning is as follows:

> Therefore, over the long span of history, the rate of population growth has tended to accelerate—almost imperceptibly at first; then slowly; and

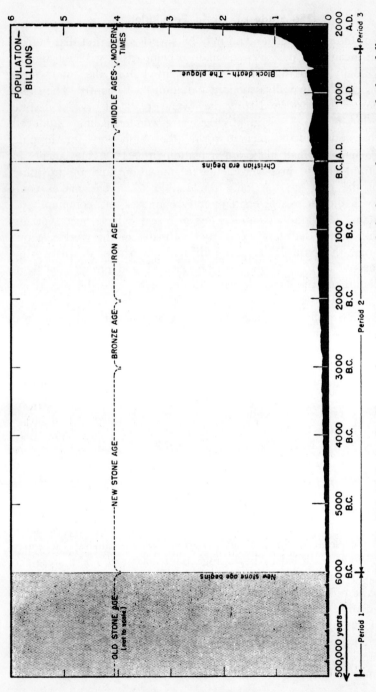

FIGURE 2.1. Growth of Human Numbers

It has taken all the hundreds of thousands of years of man's existence on earth for his numbers to reach three billion. But in only 40 more years population will grow to six billion, if current growth rates remain unchanged. If the Old Stone Age were in scale, its base line would extend 35 feet to the left!

Source: Population Reference Bureau, Inc., *Population Bulletin*, Vol. 18, No. 1 (February, 1962), p. 5. (Used by permission of the publisher.)

recently, at a rapid clip. By the beginning of the Christian era, 200-300 million people are believed to have lived on earth. That number had grown to some 500 million by 1650. Then the growth curve took a sharp upward trend. By 1850, world population was more than one billion. The quickening tempo of growth is even more dramatically expressed in doubling time. It took hundreds of thousands of years for world population to reach the quarter-billion mark, at about the beginning of the Christian era. Over 16 centuries more passed before that number reached an estimated half-billion. It took only 200 additional years to reach one billion, and only 80 more years—to about 1930—to reach two billion. Population growth rates are still going up. During all of the eons of time—perhaps as long as two million years—the human race grew to its present total of three billion. But it will take only 40 years to add the next three billion, according to United Nations estimates. In certain nations and larger areas, population will double in 25 years or even less, if growth rates remain unchanged.[1]

In considering the history of human population it is certain that, for the entire period, the numbers of people have been small as compared with figures for today. It is the distributions of the world populations of the past which are of interest to the geographer. Old settlement patterns have influenced those of today. Thus, this text reviews the progressive stages of settlement of the past and notes their arrangements.

Prehistoric Population and Settlement

Men of the Old Stone Age probably lived in small bands hardly larger than family groups. They had to be widely dispersed in order to find their food supply. Also, they had to move about over wide areas in search of game and food plants. Man is a large animal, and natural replenishment for his essential needs took time. Living was close to the resource base. The total environment was so rigorous that population growth was slow, for there was only a limited advantage of births over deaths. In consequence, human population was very sparse for hundreds of thousands of years.

As archaeologists locate the artifacts and the fossils of Paleolithic man, the scholar may be surprised at the wide distributions which are proved. Man was widely distributed over the Old World. He lived in Europe very close to the Ice-Age glacial margins, apparently in some numbers and for a long time. His record extends all the way to eastern Asia, where he was a resident of the middle latitudes. The low middle latitudes of the Old World seemed to have been favored locations. He liked the Mediterranean and was often in the natural corridors which

---

[1]Population Reference Bureau, Inc., *Population Bulletin,* Vol. 18, No. 1 (February, 1962), p. 3. (Used by permission of the publisher.)

extended in all directions from that region. Even the desert margins carry conclusive evidence that Paleolithic man used their resources. Oases were valuable territory, too, according to the records of the Middle East and North Africa. Plateau lands of eastern Africa were favorites, and the habitat extended to the margins of the southern deserts of the African continent.

The numbers of mankind must have remained below five million persons even at the close of the Old Stone Age. The population of the earlier cultural stages must have been very much smaller than those of Upper Paleolithic times. Five million people can be found living today within the boundaries of several single county areas. Also, many small countries of the world have greater total population now than the entire world contained at the close of the Paleolithic Era. Population growth was very slow during the first hundreds of thousands of years of mankind's beginnings.

The New Stone Age, graphed as beginning about 6000 B.C. on Figure 2.1, was a time during which new techniques were developed that could support a much larger population than was the case during the earlier prehistoric periods. The date of 6000 B.C. is chosen arbitrarily to represent generally the transition to a new way of life. This is an approximate date for the cultures of the Near East and the Nile Valley, but the Neolithic actually started at different times at different places over the world. Even today there are population groups which have not advanced far beyond their Paleolithic pattern of living. Generalizations such as the present one count very few people as being present in the New World. The records are for the other hemisphere.

The New Stone Age was a period during which there developed some stability to the patterns of settlement and to the ways of life for the world's human inhabitants. Favorable sites for habitation became locations for Neolithic communities. In many of these locations, stable communities were organized, some of them on sites on which have continued the settlement patterns of today. Habitations were built, and a basic agriculture was begun. Domestication of plants and animals provided a much more dependable food supply than could be provided by Paleolithic hunters. Fibers were available from both animal and plant sources. Men became craftsmen as well as hunters. In addition to their building they invented pottery, basketry, weaving, and methods of storing food. Eventually there could be the institutional development of urban centers, both the buildings and the social organization. Within this period also came other problems and institutions. Trade and exchange of goods among communities developed, slowly at first and then on a more elaborate scale. Group rivalry came, as did warfare, and conquered peoples, and slavery as an institution. Initiated during the Neolithic was the use of conquered people for building public works. Tools became specialized; they were constructed for specific uses such as for hunting, for husbandry, and for warfare. The human world needed better tools than the two stone-age periods could provide.

The long period of time graphed as the Old Stone Age and the New Stone Age, Figure 2.1, spanned thousands of centuries. That period of prehistory in its duration overshadows completely the six millennia or so of later time which is considered the time of recorded history. The archaeological record, of course, provides an even earlier overview of the story of human endeavor. Settlements were evolving into structured forms and into basic distributions. More people entered the world, and there were more contacts of population groups with one another. It was an Old-World settlement, by and large, preceding the settlement of the historical and classical periods to come afterwards. The Americas had some human population late in the period, with their record beginning at a much later time than for Afro-Eurasian land mass. Estimates of their population size near the close of the period will be included in some of the tables which are included in this chapter. As ordinarily viewed, however, the Paleolithic and the Neolithic records of human settlement are best worked out for the Old World.

Early Historic Settlement

With the beginnings of the ages of Metals, man was able to create an entirely different form of settlement. So it was that during the Bronze Age and the ensuing Iron Age true civilization really began. The historic period began late in those Ages, too, in the centuries just preceding and immediately following the beginning of the Christian Era (Figure 2.1). Population increased, and the areas of settlement extended beyond the favored locations chosen by Neolithic men.

With metal tools man was able to control his environment to a much higher degree than ever before. Population increased accordingly when man acquired his new advantages, and more territory was needed for his settlements. There came to be highly organized patterns to his growing communities. More people needed more room, and new settlements were made in new areas. They were organized in form and in function to serve the needs of overall population growth and to contribute to parent communities. Usually they were adjacent to the older centers where population concentrations had been long established. However, a very significant movement was to be noted as migrations led from the outer low latitudes to the higher latitudes which contained the great grasslands. That source of food for domesticated animals was an important element in the spread of settlement. Again, metal tools were a boon to those human groups who used animals for riding and for draft or who lived by keeping flocks of grazing animals.

Human population may have measured as 200 to 300 million by the beginning of the Christian Era. Thus, during the period between 3000 B.C. when the ages of metals began and the A.D. era, mankind must have tripled or quadrupled in numbers. Especially during the thousand years preceding the birth of Christ, there was a great acceleration in the growth of population. Significantly, it was during the later part of this period that recorded history began. The Classical Age was underway with the growing states of the Mediterranean and the Middle East colonizing and extending their empires. Many outposts were established in western and northern Europe, in central and southern Asia, and in northern Africa. The Bronze Age and the Iron Age led into the historic period. Both a growth in the total population of the Western World and an extension of the patterns of human settlement accompanied the periods. The Orient remained aloof, for the most part, making a mighty growth in the great river valleys of China. Infrequently, caravan routes permitted some contacts with their western contemporaries.

Use of metals permitted man of the early historic period to achieve in every phase of his endeavor. He had tools with which he could build, whether in wood or in stone. He had metals for making weapons suitable for war and for conquest of peoples. He had tools for the hunter, the husbandman, and the agriculturalist. Agriculture flourished; even extensive irrigation was possible. Land boundaries were laid out and described, for there were systems of measurement. Roads were planned and constructed. Domestic animals became beasts of burden and of draft. There were vehicles for land travel, for war purposes, and for cartage. Man could and did build ships. Coastal and ocean trade routes were established to supplement the land routes for local and caravan use.

The increase in population caused an enlargement of the nuclei of settlement in the area of the Classical World. At the core of each nucleus there was most often a great city. Some cities were centers of great oasis-like settlements; there were cities at the intersections of caravan routes; and there were great port cities. Outpost settlements were built, some were "colonies" of the older settlements, others were military outposts. In all of these various types of cities there were highly organized political and administrative systems. Also, highly developed social organizations evolved, with corresponding social institutions and patterns of living. Architecture during the times came to a very high stage of development. The buildings and styles of the structures were and are some of the finest the world has ever known. Along with such material developments came the development of alphabets and writing, so written records of all kinds were made possible. This last may well be the greatest improvision of all, since there has been possible since that time an accurate historical record.

The records of many empires and civilizations have been preserved, even though the communities themselves flourished in their time and later were destroyed. History records in detail the achievements and the greatness of many past communities and civilizations. The story of their wars and conquests are well told. The records are not as precise as historians need them to be; however, when they are held responsible for giving the numbers and the distributions of peoples and populations of the past. Research workers have had to work with a great deal of patience to derive reasonable estimates for population statistics during the long period of early historic time.

During the period of the Bronze Age and the Iron Age there were four faovred locations where human settlements flourished. *First* is Mesopotamia, with the Tigris and Euphrates valleys, extended by the "Fertile Crescent" northward to Anatolia, and then curving southwestward along the eastern Mediterranean shores. *Second* is the Nile Valley and its delta, with adjacent lands on both the east and west of the Red Sea, the Arabian Peninsula and Africa. *Third* is the Indus River valley of the Indian Sub-Continent, which held some great settlements. Cities like Mohenjo-Daro and Harappa in the Punjab and farther south in the Indus Valley are being studied today, like those centers of the settlements farther west. The Indus Valley had great centers of civilization. Furthermore, there were well established trade and communication contacts with other famous world cities of the period. *Fourth* is the Yangtse Valley of China and the Hwang Ho to the north, which during many centuries, carried a great population. In that region, too, great cities came to rise and decline. The Orient developed its high civilization almost independently, making few contacts with the other three great centers of settlement. A great area of settlement evolved in Southeast Asia, in the tropical setting there, with hardly any contact with the western centers. Not linked at all with the civilizations of the Old World, there were two centers of high culture already evolved in the Americas by the time of the beginning Christian Era. Settlements in Yucatan, the central plateau of Mexico, and the northern and central Andes were forerunners of the Maya, Aztec, and Inca empires, which flourished before the European conquests.

During the Classical Age, settlement moved west and northward from the Levant toward the Mediterranean Littoral. The centers of settlement during the Classical Age were in the middle latitudes, where Greece and Rome dominated the region. From their centers on the peninsulas of the northern Mediterranean and the island settlements, their influences extended widely to Africa, India, and even to Central Asia. Also, contacts and conquests were made farther north into Europe and to the extreme western and northwest territories of the European peninsulas and islands.

Dominance of the great states of the Mediterranean region on world history is very well substantiated. Gradually, after the first movement to the west and north into the higher middle latitudes, European settlement gained in relative importance. The growth of European populations outran those of the Levant. The record of western settlement became the record of Europe and European-dominated population groups. TABLE 2.1 records the distribution of population in the parts of the Roman Empire while it occupied lands in three continents. This distribution shows how the shift of population has been made to the European continent during the Classical Age.

TABLE 2.1

Area and Estimates of Population of the Roman Empire, A.D. 14

	Area, Thousands of Square Miles	Population, Thousands	Persons Per Square Mile
Total Empire	1,286	54,000	41
European part	861	23,000	26
Asiatic part	256	19,500	77
African part	117	11,500	67

Source: Population Reference Bureau, Inc., *Population Bulletin*, Vol. 18, No. 1 (February, 1962), p. 9. (Used by permission of the publisher.)

The Roman Empire had a total population of 54,000,000 persons at the time of its greatest territorial extent. As shown in TABLE 2.1, the population of the European territory was by far the greatest in the Empire, accounting for nearly half of the total. Despite its newness in comparison with the settlement of the Levant, it is apparent that the more humid lands to the north were destined to outrun the population growth of the Mediterranean littoral. An interesting comparison is to note that the population of the entire Roman Empire matched the present population of France. That country has an area of about 213,000 square miles, only one-sixth the size of the mighty empire of Rome for the year 14 A.D. It seems incredible today as one compares the small populations of the early historic times and their mighty achievements. The evidences of great cities with magnificent public buildings, as those in ruins at Persipolis in Iran or those of Carthage in present Tunisia, are the more remarkable for their historic record.

Settlement During the Christian Era, to 1600 A.D.

During this long period of historic time the earth's population doubled. From the estimated 200-300 million people at its beginning, human numbers increased to a half billion. The greater part of the gain came after 1000 A.D. as Europeans took over a dominant role in the extension of settlement. They filled their own continent, and they eventually established settlements on every continent other than Antarctica; they had initial colonies on most of the continents by 1650. They had made good use of their one hundred fifty years of the Age of Discoveries, as they perfected their program of colonization. So thoroughly did they plan their settlement abroad that they had political and economic control established for many countries and territories. The patterns of settlement of the entire world was influenced by Europeans and European management.

There was considerable growth of population in Europe during the first centuries after the birth of Christ. Figure 2.1 has presented that period as one of major changes. The period saw the extension of the Roman Empire into Europe and the increase in numbers of the indigenous peoples of the northern part of that continent. Then came a decline. There probably is a significant relationship between the end of Roman dominance and the time of Europe's Dark and Middle Ages. Those periods were noteworthy for famine, for disease epidemics, and for unstable governments which brought harsh living conditions to the population. The fall of cities in southern Europe, which had been great during the Classical Era, contributed to population losses. For example, Rome in its ascendancy is believed to have had a population of 350,000. By 500 A.D. its total number seems to have been no more than 30,000. The cities of feudal Europe were not great, either. London and Paris, the metropoli of later centuries, must have been no larger than moderate sized cities today or than contemporary Mediterranean cities which were in such sharp decline.

Records of population changes in the world's major subdivisions were even more obscure than in the European region which has the best historical record of any continent. India and China had great cities. There were well established caravan routes serving the interior of Asia. Hundreds of village settlements housed the people, for that form of settlement emerged early in the Orient. Cultural progress there was far greater than Europeans knew. Marco Polo, late in the period, used land routes for his travels. He brought back to southern Europe wondrous accounts of places he had visited. This was at the time that European explorers were making their first voyages to the coastal points of entry. The agricultural base and the social structure of the Orient were well organized at the time Europeans made their appearance.

There have been mighty kingdoms in Africa since pre-Roman times. Again, caravan routes were well laid out, providing access to North Africa and its coastal settlements with the interior. Some routes crossed the Sahara. The east side of the continent had settlements which has contacts with upper Egypt and the settlements of the Red Sea borders. Also, in the New World the Americas had great nodes of civilization in the plateau area of central Mexico and in the northern Andes. Though their numbers of population were generally much smaller than corresponding settlements in the Old World, a few Aztec cities reached 200,000 people by the late fifteenth century. The remainder of the American continents had sparse settlements, and there was much almost-empty land.

Although the total population of the world increased during the first thousand years after the birth of Christ, the numbers of gain were very small considering the long time interval. Figure 2.1 shows fluctuations within that time. Major gains and losses occurred as the scene of dominance moved to the European continent. Very significantly, Europeans never outnumbered the peoples of the Orient, but their domination of the patterns of settlement came because of their urge to explore, to colonize, and to dominate new lands.

The population changes of the next 600 years after 1000 A.D. were more significant than during the preceding period. World population doubled during that time and seemed to establish the pattern of growth for modern and later times. The changes in population for the world and its major subdivisions are summarized effectively by M. K. Bennett in a table he has prepared for his book, *The World's Food*. That table is presented here as TABLE 2.2.

TABLE 2.2

Approximate Population of the World and Its Subdivisions,
1000–1600 (in millions)

Year	World	Europe	Asiatic Russia	South West Asia	India	China Major*	Japan	South East Asia, Oceania	Africa	The Americas
1000	275	42	5	32	48	70	4	11	50	13
1100	306	48	6	33	50	79	6	12	55	17
1200	348	61	7	34	51	89	8	14	61	23
1300	384	73	8	33	50	99	11	15	67	28
1400	373	45	9	27	46	112	14	16	74	30
1500	446	69	11	29	54	125	16	19	82	41
1600	486	89	13	30	68	140	20	21	90	15

*China proper, plus Manchuria and Korea, Outer Mongolia, Sinkiang and Formosa.

Source: Population Reference Bureau, Inc., *Population Bulletin*, Vol. 18, No. 1 (February, 1962), p. 10. (Used by permission of the publisher.)
Credit is given for the table to M. K. Bennett, *The World's Food*, (New York: Harper and Brothers, 1954).

World population grew from 275 to 486 million during six hundred years, 1000 to 1600 A.D. Several important features and relationships and settlement trends are evident from the statistics of the separate subdivisions recorded by Dr. Bennett. Estimates for China show a population growth that doubled during 600 years. Also, that country has a share of one-fourth of the world's people in 1000 A.D. A high rate of growth, unaffected by Western influence, brought the totals for China's people to more than one-third of the world population by the year 1600 A.D. Other Asiatic subdivisions grew rapidly, too, so that all of the Oriental peoples together accounted for more than sixty percent of the earth's residents. Japan was noteworthy in that its small population of four million at the start of the period grew five-fold. India and Southwest Asia, by contrast, grew quite slowly during the time interval.

Europe's record of population growth between 1000 and 1600 A.D. was distinctive among those of the world's major subdivisions. In total, that continent gained population from 42 million to 89 million during the period. However, the figures record a significant setback during that time. By 1300, the population number had gained to 73 millions, but it declined during the fourteenth century to only 45 million persons. At mid-century the bubonic plague struck with such severity that as many as one-fourth of the population of some countries may have died during the epidemic. Gain was rapid later, so that within the next two hundred years the population doubled. This rapid growth came during the centuries that Europe began to progress into its modern period of history.

Other major subdivisions have interesting records of population growth, too. Africa, generally quite remote from European influence during the time period, had a total population gain that matched that of Europe. The gain was gradual, not marked by a sharp upswing like that of Europe. Asiatic Russia gained rapidly in numbers, although it has a small population total even at the close of the period. The third major subdivision remote from Europe was the Americas. TABLE 2.2 shows a modest population number of 13 million for 1000 A.D. and then a tripling of that number by 1500, when the first contacts came with Europeans. Then, remarkably, the first century of European occupation brought a decline from 41 to only 15 million persons. Although European authority was very cruel to the natives of the western continents, most population losses resulted from European-introduced diseases. Measles and smallpox took the heartiest toll.

Another research study provides a different estimate of the numbers of the indigenous populations of the Americas as they were first contacted by European explorers. Dr. Julian Steward has offered estimates

of the Indian population distribution in different regions of the New
World in 1492 by the following tabulation:[2]

> North America:
>   North of Mexico 1,000,000
>   Mexico 4,500,000
>   West Indies 225,000
>   Central America 736,000
> South America:
>   Andean Area 6,131,000
>   Remainder 2,898,000
>   Total 15,490,000

Although the total numbers given by Dr. Bennett and Dr. Steward
are severely at variance, the statistics emphasize the importance of the
mid-portions of the New World for the indigenous peoples. The importance of the Mexican highlands and of the Andean region is very
evident, with their areas containing more than two-thirds of the people
of the continents. By adding to these two communities the nearby settlements of northern South America, Central America, and the West
Indies, most of the population of the Americas is accounted for. North
America especially was very thinly settled when Europeans began their
program of exploration, conquest, and colonization.

World Population Distribution, 1650 A.D.

The year 1650 is a date for which research workers have prepared
some very comprehensive estimates of population. It was an important
year because by that date the world's people numbered a half billion.
It was a year at which time censuses were being considered by European countries. Also, the modern period was under way. Europeans
were putting their own continent to work. They were organizing colonial systems for new lands, and many colonies were already established. Furthermore, a technological program was being started at
home, and a system of utilizing the resources of distant lands was beginning so Europe could be the center of a colonial and a trading
world.

The work of three research workers who have prepared estimates
for the world's population in 1650 is summarized in TABLE 2.3. These
data extend the record, presented in TABLE 2.2, which recorded the
progressive changes in population growth from the year 1000 A.D. A
significant added element in the new table is the record of European
settlement.

[2]Source: Population Reference Bureau, Inc., *Population Bulletin*, Vol. 18, No. 1
(February, 1962), p. 12. (Used by permission of the publisher.)

Table 2.3
Estimated World Population by Regions, 1650
Millions of People

World Region	Estimates by Demographers			
	Carr-Saunders	Wilcox	Reuther	
			Population	Per Cent
World	545	470	465	100%
Africa	100	100	100	21.5
N. America	1	1	7*	1.5
Latin America	12	7	6*	1.3
Asia (Esc. USSR)	327	257	250†	53.8
Europe and USSR	103	103	100†	21.5
Oceania	2	2	2	0.4
Areas of European‡ Settlement	118	113	No Estimate Given	

*Reuter uses South America and North America as his regional divisions. This system in effect transfers the population estimates for Mexico and the Caribbean areas to North America.

†The boundaries of Europe and Asia are considered as the Urals. Thus Asiatic Russia is included in Asia, according to Reuter.

‡"Areas of European Settlement" include northern America, Latin America, Europe and the Asiatic USSR, and Oceania.

Source: Data adapted from two sources.
   Population Reference Bureau, Inc., *Population Bulletin*, Vol. 18, No. 1 (February, 1962), p. 13. (Used by permission of the publisher.)
   Edward B. Reuter, *Population Problems*, 2nd ed. (New York: J. B. Lippincott Company, 1937), p. 36. (Used by permission of Mrs. Edward B. Reuter.)

Tabulated statistics for the individual continental areas have some important meanings for an interpretation of the world's settlement at mid-seventeenth century. Asia had considerably more than half of the world's peoples or sixty percent according to Carr-Saunders' estimate. Africa's population exceeded that of Europe, when the twelve million or so of Asiatic Russia's peoples were subtracted. Oceania had only a few people but even at that the number was double the figure estimated for North America. Again, the Americas have an interesting summary, with differences in categories making an apparent discrepancy among the tables of the three statisticians. Reuter grouped the population of Mexico and Middle America, and the Antilles with North America. Thus, while Latin America had originally a large population of indigenous peoples there were already many Europeans in the region. North America north of the Rio Grande, the traditional northern boundary of Latin America, had hardly begun to receive its later-arriving great numbers of European colonists. North America's Indian population was located in only a few favored sections; coastal strips, river valleys, favored woodlands, and in oasis-like sites in the mid-section of the continent. More or less permanent communities were located on the

Pacific coast littoral, forming one of the most highly organized settlements on the continent.

Europeans who resided in their own continent in 1650, numbered about one hundred million. The added category, "Areas of European Settlement," holds much significance for the geographer interested in population distribution at this period. Besides the residents of Europe and the territory of the present U.S.S.R., Carr-Saunders estimated that there were already fifteen million people of European extraction living in Latin America, North America, Asiatic U.S.S.R., and Oceania. Willcox made a lower estimate, with his figures showing ten million European transplanted as colonists and then continuing as established residents of other continents. All of this transplanted settlement has taken place within the first 150 years of the period of exploration and planting of colonies on distant soil.

World Population Growth, 1650-1850

Since 1650 the records of human population have been more meaningful and more nearly accurate than for earlier periods. Most countries have censuses now and have taken them for many years. Some fairly well documented records go back almost to the start of the period under discussion. Lately the United Nations has given great assistance to the program. Their *Demographic Yearbook* and special studies and reports on population are the most complete records that have ever been made. It is appropriate that their estimates and tabulations be used to supplement the work of earlier demographers.

A basic table on population growth trends by world regions has been prepared from the works of demographers for the earlier periods and from United Nations sources for the last decades. That statistical summary is presented here as TABLE 2.4. It brings the record up-to-date for the graphic presentation offered early in the study as Figure 2.1. The present table is used in this section to document the changes in world settlement during 1650-1850 and also to highlight the basic growth trends after that period until the 1960 census.

The numbers of human population doubled between 1650 and 1850. The earlier date was one on which for the first time there was a half billion residents of the earth. Two hundred years later there were a billion people in the world. Remembering that the time from the birth of Christ to 1650 was required to double the world's population from the quarter billion number of that earlier time span, it is apparent that the more of the rapid gains occurred within later historic times. A doubling during modern times took only two centuries. It had taken sixteen centuries before, with the major part of the growth after 1000

Table 2.4

Estimates of World Population by Regions, 1650-1960
Estimated Population in Millions

Source of estimates and date	World	Africa	Northern America[a]	Latin America[b]	Asia (excl. USSR)[c]	Europe and Asiatic USSR[c]	Oceania	Area of European Settlement[d]
Willcox's estimates:								
1650	470	100	1	7	257	103	2	113
1750	694	100	1	10	437	144	2	157
1800	919	100	6	23	595	193	2	224
1850	1,091	100	26	33	656	274	2	335
1900	1,571	141	81	63	857	423	6	573
Carr-Saunders' estimates:								
1650	545	100	1	12	327	103	2	118
1750	728	95	1	11	475	144	2	158
1800	906	90	6	19	597	192	2	219
1850	1,171	95	26	33	741	274	2	335
1900	1,608	120	81	63	915	423	6	573
United Nations estimates:								
1920	1,810	140	117	91	966	487	9	704
1930	2,013	155	135	109	1,072	532	10	786
1940	2,246	172	146	131	1,212	573	11	861
1950	2,495	200	167	163	1,376	576	13	919
1960	2,972	244	200	207	1,665	641	16	1,064

[a]United States, Canada, Alaska, St. Pierre and Miquelon.
[b]Central and South America and Caribbean Islands.
[c]Estimates for Asia and Europe in Willcox's and Carr-Saunders' series have been adjusted so as to include the population of the Asiatic USSR with that of Europe.
[d]Includes northern America, Latin America, Europe and the Asiatic USSR and Oceania.

Source: Population Reference Bureau, Inc., *Population Bulletin.* Vol. 18, No. 1 (February, 1962), p. 13. (Used by permission of the publisher.)

A.D. It is the acceleration of growth that has caught the interest of both demographers and historians. The emerging geographic patterns which have emerged in the growing settlement are of special significance for the population geographer. What are the characteristics and distributions of modern settlement?

Several factors entered into the rapid growth of world population during the 1650-1850 period. First of all, there was an extension of European settlement. As Table 2.4 shows, there were 61 million people of European stock living in continents other than Europe by 1850, equaling more than a fifth of the total population of the "mother continent." The latter part of the time interval, from about 1750 to 1850, was the beginning of the Industrial Revolution. Even at the outset, as is true for all later time, the mechanization of manufacturing and industrial processes has profoundly affected the distribution of settlement.

A third factor of special importance, as the rapid growth of population began, was the trend to urbanization. There developed a form of livelihood for extra people who moved to great cities and then were able to support themselves there. An estimated 50.4 million people lived in cities of 20,000 and larger in 1850. This was 4.3 percent of the world's total population of 1,171,000,000 for that date.[3] Urbanization had begun, a trend which has increased as population has doubled and then almost redoubled within the most recent century. The time period after 1850 is one in which the rise of cities is the major phenomenon of human settlement.

Growth of population within the different world regions occurred at very different rates during the 1650-1850 period. Asia's peoples numbered 327 million in 1650 and 741 million in 1850. This was a percentage gain of 126.7 percent for the continent. Significantly, the population comprised more than 63.3 percent of the world's population total. Two-thirds of the earth's peoples lived on the Asian land mass in 1850. The scattered population of Siberia must be considered as a part of Asia's totals. Africa did not gain population during the two centuries. Despite the establishment of many European settlements on the continent, there was a loss in the numbers of indigenous peoples. Nor did the region of Australia and other lands included in Oceania gain population. The estimated two million population there in 1850 indicated that very few Europeans had become a part of the settlement.

Population changes of Europe and of the Americas during the 1650-1850 period represent strikingly the extension of European settlement. The European continent (and Asiatic U.S.S.R.) gained 171 million people, increasing from the initial total of 103 million to 274 million. This was a population gain of 166 percent; meanwhile, the continent was exporting a tremendous number of people to other continents and to colonies. The Americas were accepting many of Europe's migrating people. North America was principally involved in this movement; with a very small indigenous population at the outset, there was wide-open space for European immigrants. In 1650, North America had an estimated one million population. By 1850 the total had grown to 26 million. Latin America, which had the greater share of the American Indian population at the outset, made a large gain, too. In 1650 the region had a population of 12 million people (Carr-Saunders, TABLE 2.4) a number which increased by 1850 to 33 million. The gain of 21 million, or 175 percent, was a very high rate for an already settled area. By 1850, the Americas had their patterns of European settlement well established.

---

[3] Population Reference Bureau, Inc., *Population Bulletin*, Vol. 16, No. 6 (September, 1960), p. 114. This percentage is shown in an article, "World's Great Cities."

The extension of European settlement is a striking phenomenon of the change in the world's population during modern times. In 1650, as has been shown, ten million Europeans were living as transplanted settlers in other world regions. By 1850, 335 million peoples of European descent were listed, one-third of the world's total population. Besides the 274 million people living in Europe itself there were 61 million living abroad. This number more than equals the combined population totals given for North America and Latin America for that date. The first flush of colonization and its influences were past. European settlers were established on every continent by 1850, with their corresponding effects on political, economic, and physical structures of the settlement.

World Population Growth After 1850

The record of population and human settlement is more distinct for the time period after 1850 than for before that date. Censuses have been taken in much of the world, and demographers have been able to derive reliable estimates for the other areas. Furthermore, statistical devices have been worked out so that prediction of population growth for the future is done very accurately. The rate of growth of population is a phenomenon of the most recent decades, with the whole world alerted to the "population explosion" which is taking place.

Rapid growth of population during the most recent hundred years is a crucial part of the story of human settlement. In 1850, for the first time, there were a billion people to be counted on the earth. The preceding section has pointed out that the time of doubling the total number to gain that total took two hundred years from the time when colonial programs were being established in 1650 until 1850 when the political structures of most modern countries were well established. Later, bringing the record into contemporary times, one can note that human population doubled again by 1930, TABLE 2.4. Only eighty years were required to make the statistical point, rather than two hundred years for the same item in the earlier instance. The world had one and a half billion population in 1900, then gained another half billion during the first three decades of the twentieth century.

It is appropriate to note the distributions of population in 1930, the first date on which two billion people lived in the world. More than half of the total lived in Asia, which had more than a billion people. Europe has half as many, with 532 million living in that continent and in Asiatic U.S.S.R., TABLE 2.4. Africa had gained about sixty million population, and Oceania was accepting a large number of new settlers who soon outnumbered indigenous people, with ten million residents in Australia and island groups. North America's population growth

outran Latin America's during the eighty years, with their 1930 populations recorded as 135 and 109 millions, respectively. North America
had accepted a mighty flood of European immigrants during the last
three decades before 1900, as it did later after the turn of the century.
That component of the population far outnumbered the migrants to
Latin America during the same time. The difference between the population listed as "Area of European Settlement," 786 million for 1930,
and the population of Europe and Asiatic U.S.S.R., 532 million, is 254
million persons. That number of European stock is greater than the
combined population figures given for the Americas. Colonialism was
a mighty institution, and the European components of population added
by the long program were established in all of the world's major regions
before and during the early decades of the twentieth century.

After 1930, when the world had two billion people, the population
growth has accelerated so that a real "population explosion" has been a
realization. There has been a great increase in numbers of people on
every continent. Urbanism has become the order in every populous
region and in the least densely settled communities, too. There has
been a general decline in the death rates everywhere. In many instances
where birth rates have declined, they have not kept even with the de-
clining death rates. Some ideas of sanitation, immunization from diseases, advanced medical practices, and improved agriculture that has
brought a greater food supply than has ever been available before
have contributed to an increased life expectancy in almost every part of
the world. As the numbers of people increase, there is constant need
for increased supplies of food and for technological opportunities for
a population which must have employment. The world's population in
1960 was approaching three billion, and the estimates for 1968 show
that nearly three and a half billion people now live on the earth.

It is not an idle statistical forecast that there will be four billion
people on earth by the early 1970's. The doubling of the given numbers
of population which this study has presented through the respective
time intervals is an even more important matter today than ever before.
Preceding the 1930 milestone, it had taken eighty years to double the
population. Presently it is almost a certainty that a forty-year time
span will repeat the same statistical event. The acceleration of population increase shown in Figure 2.1 is being realized for the decades
between 1930 and the present. Nor is the extension beyond the present
to the year 2000 A.D. an unreasonable prediction.

Regional distribution of the world's population during the 1960's
carries a great deal of meaning in an analysis of the pattern of contemporary human settlement. TABLE 2.4 carries the United Nations estimates for each decade after 1920. Growth in population numbers for

the major world regions and the relative sizes of their populations are documented. Asia's population constitutes more than half of the world's peoples. Africa's numbers continued to grow very rapidly. Oceania remained sparsely populated, considering numbers comparatively, although making a high percentage gain. Europe seemed to have stabilized with its population gain, losing ground relatively with most other regions. The Americas changed roles during the 1930-1960 period, with Latin America having, at the end of the thirty-year period, seven million greater total population than its northern neighbor. The rapid growth of people in that region is one of the most noteworthy trends observed anywhere among the population records. Again, as in former sections of this study, the extension of population in the "Area of European Settlement" is significant. There were 423 million of European stock and their descendants in continents other than Europe by 1960. That number was included and assimilated within the population of every major region of the world.

Population Forecasts

It is possible to predict with a great deal of accuracy the growth of population during the decades of the immediate future. Population will number more than six billion people by 2000 A.D. This is double the number reached during the early 1960's. A forecast made by the United Nations statisticians in 1958 has been used as the basis of a table prepared to show the estimated population growth by continents by 25-year periods for the twentieth century. TABLE 2.5 shows those predictions with tabulations using the same regional divisions that have been included in TABLES 2.3 and 2.4 of this study.

Asia in 2000 A.D. will have 61.8 percent of the world's people. That proportion has been gaining during most of the century. Europe's change is an increase in total numbers, but a decline relatively to 15.1 percent of the total. Africa and Oceania will gain population at the same rates they have been following during recent decades. North America has passed its period of exceptionally rapid growth and may expect to have only five percent of the world's people by 2000 A.D. Latin America is expected to continue a sharp upswing that began at mid-century. The forecasted 592 million population, more than the present population of Western Europe today and more than double Latin America's present population of the mid-1960's, is an exceptionally significant element among the coming shifts in settlement. By 2000 A.D. Latin America will have more people than Africa, the other great continent of the lower latitudes but one with a much larger land area than the American region.

TABLE 2.5

Estimated Population of Continents and Population Projections, 1900-2000

	1900		1925		1950		1975		2000	
	Mil- lions	Per Cent	Mil- lions	Per Cent	Mil- lions	Per Cent	Mil- lions	Per Cent	Mil- lions	Per Cent
Europe and USSR	423	27.3	505	26.5	574	23.0	751	19.6	947	15.1
Northern America*	81	5.2	126	6.6	168	6.7	240	6.3	312	5.0
Oceania	6	0.4	10	0.5	13	0.5	21	0.5	29	0.5
Latin America	63	4.1	99	5.2	163	6.5	303	7.9	592	9.4
Asia	857	55.3	1,020	53.5	1,380	55.2	2,210	57.7	3,870	61.8
Africa	120	7.7	147	7.7	199	8.0	303	7.9	517	8.2
World	1,550	100.0	1,907	100.0	2,497	100.0	3,828	100.0	6,267	100.0

*"That is America north of Mexico"

Source: William Petersen, *Population*, © 1961, p. 501. The Macmillan Company. New York. (Used by permission of the publisher.)
Petersen's source as indicated for his table is: United Nations, Department of Economic and Social Affairs, *The Future Growth of World Population* (Population Studies, No. 28; New York, 1958), pp. 23, 24.

A tabulation by the Population Reference Bureau, entitled "World Population Data Sheet—1968," gives some very significant data which add details to population forecasts. Data in TABLE 2.6 are offered to show the background for some comparative estimates.

TABLE 2.6

POPULATION ESTIMATES FOR WORLD REGIONS, MID-1968

Population in Millions

World Region	Population 1968	Years required to double population
World	3,479	35 yrs.
Africa	333	31
North America	222	63
Latin America	268	24
Asia (Exc. USSR)	1,943	32
Europe	455	100
USSR	239	63
Oceania	18.5	39

Source: Population Reference Bureau, Inc., Information Service, "World Population Data Sheet—1968," Washington, D. C., March, 1968. (Used by permission of the publisher.)

Europe's population is the slowest growing of any region. Both North America and the U.S.S.R., for which data are given separately here, will require 63 years to double their present population numbers. Latin America has the most rapidly growing population of any world region, so its population may be expected to double within a single generation. Only a little more than that length of time will be required to double the population of Asia and Africa. Those two continents have always been high in the population totals, and both have different forms of settlement from that of the Western World. In the future, even more than in the past and present, their numbers will gain relatively in comparison among world regions.

In summary, for the growth of human population during the time span of 1000 years, from 1000 A.D. until 2000 A.D., a most remarkable graph has been prepared by the Population Reference Bureau. That graph presents by a set of "pie diagrams" several highly significant generalizations that have been taken from the statistics on the growing world population. The page is reproduced here as Figure 2.2 to sum up the major trends which have been noted through time, and in regions, as human settlement has been developed through the latest thousand years of historic time.

First of all, the giant population of Asia is noted, as it has dominated the total numbers of settlement during all the time period. In 1800, the proportion of the world's people on the Asian land mass was the greatest of that for any date shown. It is significant that Asia's share of the totals for both 1900 and 1960 was smaller than is projected for 2000 A.D. This is the same point made by TABLE 2.5, which records growth in percentages. Europe has long been a strong contender for a place in the world's population record. For the dates shown, however, the graph for 1900 is the only one which shows Europe as having more than one-fourth of the world's people. The Americas have grown during the centuries since the Age of Discoveries and with the extension of European settlement. The great increase now taking place in Latin America, more than for its northern neighbor, accounts for the large shaded areas on the graphs for the two latest time periods. Africa has had a substantial growth through the centuries, perhaps with the most uniform rate of increase of any continent. This has been the rule despite the colonization of Europeans and the immigrants from other continents, particularly from Asia. One may speculate on what will happen to Africa's peoples during a yet later time. Will the growth rate continue, and will it increase in time with a boom similar to that of Latin America during the present generation?

Having the world so full of people as at present is a new problem which has come to the human race within the present generation. A billion people have been added to the world's settled areas within the last forty years, bringing problems of every kind which must be solved very soon. The upward spiral is increasing, so that adults today may well witness the growth to six billion people as they participate in the world's planning and living structures. Already the shifting pattern of settlement has created a vast array of great cities housing and employing millions of inhabitants. From 1800, when there were 2.4 percent of the world population living in cities, the proportion increased to 20.9 percent for 1950. These millions of people lived in cities of

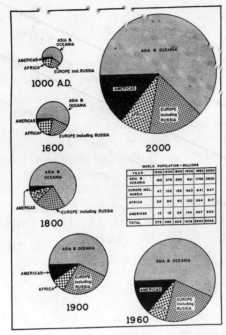

WORLD POPULATION – MILLIONS						
YEAR	1000	1600	1800	1900	1960	2000
ASIA & OCEANIA	165	279	599	921	1700	3900
EUROPE INCL. RUSSIA	47	102	192	423	641	947
AFRICA	50	90	90	120	244	517
AMERICAS	13	15	25	144	407	904
TOTAL	275	486	906	1608	2992	6268

In 1000 A.D., Asia accounted for 60 percent of the world's population, Europe, including Russia, for about 17 percent, Africa, 18 percent and the Americas, 4 percent. By 1960, Asia's percentage had declined to somewhat under 60, that of Europe and the USSR had increased to 22 percent and the Americas, to 14 percent. Africa's portion declined to percent. By 2000, Asia may comprise about 65 percent of the total, Europe and the USSR, 15 percent, the Americas, 15 percent and Africa, 8 percent. Russia includes Asiatic and European Russia.

FIGURE 2.2. A Thousand Years of World Population Growth

Source: Population Reference Bureau, Inc., *Population Bulletin*, Vol. 18, No. 1 (February, 1962), p. 11. (Used by permission of the publisher.)

20,000 or larger. The cities will continue to grow, in size and in numbers, so that undoubtedly quite soon three-fourths of the world's people will be urban dwellers. Planning by new generations must provide a living for all.

With numerical growth of population, there has come to be an unparalleled drain on the supply of natural resources and foodstuffs needed to support the human family. The program of present decades have been distinctive in that knowledge of health measures has received a substantial and wider application. However, knowledge of limiting population growth and interest in population control have not kept up. There has been a race for the production and distribution of foods and other supplies needed so that everyone can have a satisfactory living. The record of success is not a good one. Longevity has in part been achieved, child care has improved so that mortality of the very young has been reduced, but there has not been widespread relief from the world's perennial hunger. The interest of every government today, whether of Western or Eastern persuasion, is in trying to relieve the pressures of too many people. All population groups need an opportunity for living, a constructive form of livelihood, and a share of the world's resources and its derivatives.

Geographic Bases of Human Settlement

Arrangement of human population to agree with the pattern of the earth's physical features is a relationship which a geographer may expect to find as he studies the set of world maps. Physical attributes of some world regions give particular advantages to human settlement; other environments are so restrictive that it is difficult for men to live there in more than limited numbers. When glancing at the world's population map showing how population is presently arranged, one can try to match complex forms of human settlement with the areas that offer greater advantages. Sparse settlements would be located in regions where conditions are severely restrictive. Such is not always the case, however, because many elements of human decision enter the story. Present-day patterns of world settlement with great numbers of population are a new development, as has been shown in Chapter 2. However, in many areas today, the numbers of people do not match the quality of the land nor the supply of the resources. Climaxes have not been reached. Nevertheless, at the beginning of a study of settlement, the student notes the relationships between the basic physical patterns of the world's continents and the gross patterns that are the distributions of human population. Also noted are the instances when the two distributions do not coincide.

Many world communities or countries are overcrowded, with their food supply limited by over-demand and with basic economic development lagging. An adequate living may be denied the people of those regions. Areas with sparse population may be restrictive, too, unable to provide adequately for the small settlements there. Some world communities seem to balance their resource base and their population needs adequately. A superficial survey may indicate that certain regions are capable of containing their dense populations and may be expected to support them well. For a study of world settlement, it is imperative that the set of patterns of the world's gross physical features be studied in comparison with the world's population map.

Areas with Dense Population

Approximately nine-tenths of the world's population lives upon one-fifth of the earth's land surface. Within very limited areas, population is densely concentrated. Living there is complex and often difficult. In most cases the settlement is mature, and a well organized system has been developed for use of the region's resources. The supply of arable land may be used to the limit. Any other resource may have been quite fully exploited. Livelihood is varied among these densely settled regions, so that individually each region may have its own specialization. It may be that the entire community is hard pressed to provide a good living for all of its residents. There must be an arrangement of complementary activities, too, so that the members of the entire settlement may participate in the living and sharing of the major specialization. Despite the great numbers of people in the individual settlements, each individual in his own niche, there is a high degree of individuality among the large world communities. Some of these may be noted as the areas of concentrated population are reviewed in their relationships with the world's major geographical patterns.

population distribution by continents

Three continents contain the four major concentrations of human population. *First*, Western Europe, *frontispiece*, carries a pattern of human population over most of its area. It is the most completely settled of any continent. An extension of Europe's settled area is a triangle which extends eastward beyond the traditional boundary of the Urals into western Siberia, to about 90° East Longitude. *Second*, North America has its major settled area extending from the Atlantic Seaboard westward to the 90° Meridian West and from the Great Lakes southward to the Gulf of Mexico. *Third* and *Fourth*, Asia has two great concentrations which together include half of the world's peoples, Figure 2.2. Eastern Asia, from northern Manchuria to south China and from Japan and Korea westward to the arid lands of China's interior, makes the world's greatest area of settlement. The Indian subcontinent, with India and Pakistan hemmed in by natural barriers of enclosing mountain ranges, is the setting for many millions of people of South Asia.

Other concentrations of human settlement are a great deal more restrictive in area than the four major regions just listed. Every continent has communities of dense settlement. They serve as core areas for their respective countries or regions. They are nuclei for further population growth within their own settings, and they dominate the livelihood of their communities. Southeastern Asia has several of these small and highly concentrated areas of settlement. Java is noteworthy because it has the densest population in the world in an area which has a non-industrial base. Malaya, Cambodia, Viet Nam, Burma, Ceylon, and Luzon Island (in the Philippines) all have dense populations within restrictive territorial size. Africa's population concentrations are very different from those of Asia. The lower Nile Valley of Egypt has an extremely high population density. This is concentrated in an enlarged oasis-type of settlement. Areas of West Africa, particularly in Nigeria, several limited sized sections of East and South Africa, and North Africa's coastal communities make up the others.

The population map shows the New World and Australia with several settlements which have nuclei at the periphery of the continents. South America's major concentrations extend inland from the Atlantic into Argentina-Uruguay, into Southeastern Brazil, and along the eastern coastline of Brazil. Western South America has a small densely settled area in central Chile, and there are limited areas of settlement in the northwestern and the northern countries of the continent. Mexico has a node of settlement in its interior. Western North America has a line of settlement near its western margin. Australia's new settlement is in the southeastern part of that continent, small in area and in numbers of population in comparison with most of the areas just now designated.

population distributions by latitudes

Location in latitude is an important element as a student analyzes the characteristics of settlement of the world's populated areas. Particularly in the densely settled regions is this consideration important. Basic forms of agriculture, the food supply, many of the occupations, basic activities, and the manner of living all are related to the regional location in latitude. It has been noted that exploration and colonization were practiced especially by population groups of the middle and higher latitudes. Distributions of settlement by latitude, as they are found today, offer some interesting geographical points for consideration.

Great concentrations of population in Asia are found within the latitudes of 10° to 40° North. Thus the outer "low latitudes" (Low, 0°-30°) and the lower "middle latitudes" (Middle, 30°-60°) include most of Asia's peoples. Except for the peninsula of India and Ceylon (10° North), the vast population of India, China, Japan, and Korea live within the limits of 20° and 40° North Latitude. Manchuria's vast corridor of population in its central plain extends farther north, and the northern Japanese island, Hokkaido, extends into the latitudes where severe winters are the rule. Generally, however, the living of half of the world's people may be thought of as belonging to latitudes where conditions favor more warmth than cold. The vast population of Asia lives within an area that is scarcely more than one-tenth of the area of the continent.

Most of Europe's population is located between the parallels of 40° and 60° North. This is the farthest north of the great settlements, with its greatest concentration centered at about the fiftieth parallel. Settlement on the continent which has provided the basic stock of immigrants to the areas which have become "Areas of European Settlement" is located farther from the Equator than that of any other major area.

North America's great concentration of population is in the eastern part of the continent, between 30° and 45° latitudes. This is a much smaller region than the others just named for Asia and Europe and makes up only one-sixth of the continent. It extends westward from the Atlantic seaboard to the ninetieth meridian and is the coreland of the United States and Canada. This region is the most nearly complete "Area of European Settlement" recorded in the series of tables for Chapter 2 of any major world region.

As was the case when the patterns of settlement by continent were being reviewed, there are many smaller areas of dense population than the four chief areas which show so emphatically on the world's population map. The location in latitude of these small but densely populated areas adds much to the story of the distributions of settlement.

The smaller areas of intensive settlement in the New World vary greatly in their location. Western North America has California's population located between 32° and 38° North Latitude, forming an outlier away from the eastern core of the United States that carries the greatest population of any one of the fifty states. The corelands of South America's eastern countries are nearer the Equator than those of North America, ranging from about 20° to 38° South Latitude. The most densely settled community of Brazil is nearer the Equator than the Tropic of Capricorn. Interestingly, the latitude of that concentration matches very closely that of Mexico's core community on the Central Plateau of that country north of the Equator. Western South America's settlement centers at the Equator, within 10° North or South Latitude. Colombia and Venezuela have their population concentrations within ten degrees of the Equator, while the West Indies range northward to the Tropic of Cancer. The Greater Antilles are between the twentieth parallel and the Tropic.

Locations nearer the Equator than 15° North or South Latitude offer a sharp contrast in their patterns of settlement. Very dense populations are located in Java, Malaya, and parts of Southeast Asia. Africa has population concentrations in West Africa, some of the densest of the continent. Generally, however, the regions of dense population avoid the lower latitudes.

It is interesting to speculate on how population would be arranged if there were extensive areas of continental size in the middle latitudes of the southern hemisphere. Actually both the Old World with Africa's Cape of Good Hope at 34° South and South America's pointed end of the continent extending to 55° South at Cape Horn present a very restrictive area in the middle latitudes. Australia has its widest area south of the Tropic of Capricorn, but the mainland fails to extend beyond about 39° South, a latitude that matches that of St. Louis, Missouri, in the northern hemisphere; that parallel bisects the populated area of eastern North America. Tasmania extends the Australian land mass further south to about 43°. New Zealand, southeast of the mainland, carries the land mass to nearly 47° South, a distance from the Equator that matches that of Brittany, the westernmost tip of France. Australia's population is mostly within the latitudes of 30° to 40° South, matching the latitude of the settlement of southeastern United States. That distribution corresponds also to the southern extent of the population east of the Andes of South America. However, Chile, west of that range, has a settled area projecting as far south as the southern island of New Zealand. The southern continents have little land area extending beyond the low latitudes.

The 60° Northern parallel is a significant boundary for population distribution in the North Hemisphere. Europe's concentrations of population seem almost to stop at that northern line. It is of major significance, however, that great cities and their communities are located almost exactly at that parallel. Oslo, the capital of Norway, and Stockholm, Sweden's capital near the northern part of that country's major settlement, are both at about 60° North. The second greatest city of the Soviet Union, Leningrad, is located at the 60° parallel, just at the outer limit of the "middle latitudes."

Latitude is an important element for consideration when analyzing the distributions of human settlements. The greatest areas of settlement are found in the outer limits of the low latitudes and in the middle latitudes. Many outliers are found in the low latitudes, even at the equator, as well as within all continents and all regions where there are locations favorable for settlement. The Oriental cultural areas are located nearer the Equator than the thirtieth parallel, generally, while regions of westernized settlement have distributed themselves prin-

cipally within the middle latitudes. The settlement of the European
continent is distinctive because it is at the highest latitudes of all the
major settled regions.

population distribution and major land forms

In a very accurate way, the map of the earth's land forms presents
a pattern which shows the areas that are advantageous or restrictive
for human settlement. Physical features may offer favored areas, or
they may provide barriers to the extension of population. They may
combine with latitude and with location within the major land masses
to offer special sites for settlement. They may offer corridors for ingress
and egress to locations in the continental areas. A physical map of the
world and a population map show many close relationships. Figure 3.1
delineates the arrangement of the world's major landform regions,
showing four major classes of topographic features.

The world's plains areas are the most favored sites for human settlement. The plains areas of North America and European middle latitudes are especially coveted areas which carry dense populations. Some
of the plains of the low latitudes, too, have great concentrations of
settlement. The Ganges Valley of India, for example, is one of the
world's most densely populated plains areas. Along with plains are
great river valleys. The valleys and flood plains and the valley sides
are prized locations as are the river deltas where land is at a premium
in the low and middle latitudes.

Hill country is restrictive in the numbers of population it can carry,
especially in middle or high latitudes. This land, with a local relief
of 500 to 2000 feet within the extent of a few miles and with most
of its area in slope, affords too little tillable land to support many
people. In the Orient it is a different matter. China has a high proportion of its area in hill lands in the outer low latitudes of eastern Asia.
Terracing is a way of life, so that hard hand labor must provide the
equivalent of plains on the hill slopes beside the river valleys. Elsewhere in the low latitudes the hill lands are especially sought out. The
East Indies, the Philippines, and Southeast Asia use the hill lands as
favored locations.

Plateaus (also called "high plains") are extremely interesting phenomena as they offer sites for human settlement. They are most valuable in very low latitudes. There the advantages of lower temperatures
because the elevation makes living more pleasant and increases the
health conditions for the residents. Some forms of agriculture and horticulture are practiced in low latitude plateau areas which are impossible
for lower lying plains or river valley and delta locations. Southeastern
Brazil is an example, for near the coast the plateau rises to a height

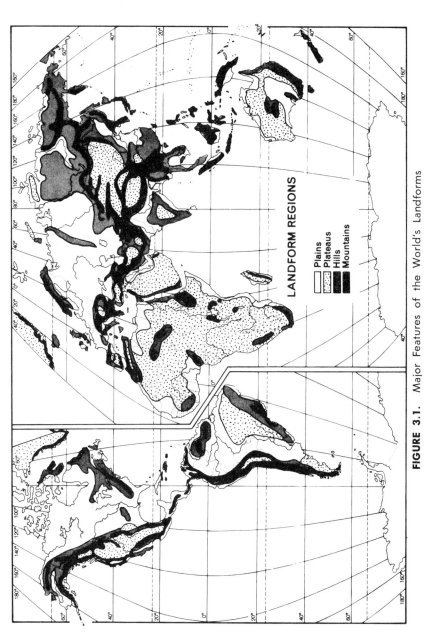

FIGURE 3.1. Major Features of the World's Landforms

LANDFORM REGIONS

- Plains
- Plateaus
- Hills
- Mountains

Source: Joseph Bixby Hoyt, *Man and the Earth*, 2nd ed., © 1967, p. 94. Reprinted by permission of Prentice-Hall, Inc., Englewood Cliffs, New Jersey.

where the temperature range is more pleasant and favored coffee land country is provided as well. The heart of Mexico's settlement is the central plateau of the country, where the nation's capital is located. The location is at about 20° North Latitude at an elevation of 7000 feet.

Plateau areas most often are restrictive to movements of people within their region. Valleys may be deeply incised and crossings difficult. If there are to be bridges, they are expensive and hard to build. If there are rivers with steep valley sides, they are swift and unsuited for navigation. The erosion rate for agricultural land is rapid in a dissected plateau, so that frequently the land is impoverished by use. Since they are usually inland from the borders of their own land masses, plateaus tend to be remote in terms of access by normal transportation routes.

Mountain areas are the most restrictive topographical features of all. In almost all cases the world maps showing mountains and population distribution present these regions as nearly devoid of inhabitants. When the scale of the maps is enlarged it can be noted that there are many settled communities in mountain areas, some of them quite large. They may be located where there is a mineral to be mined or where there is a favored basin-like area that provides a section of fairly level land. Settlements are made in passes or at gateways or at crossing points of routes along the mountains and in valleys. Routeways are difficult to find and expensive to provide in mountain regions. It is not unusual for routes to wind for long instances to get to favored passes or to oasis stops which provide a way-stop or something of particular interest to the traveler. These tortuous routes serve both the residents of the mountain community and the travelers from outside the region. Mountains have become with time one of the most effective boundaries of all for dividing communities of human settlers. They have very often been converted through long use to political boundaries.

Lesser landform features than the four major classes are of very great importance in the distributions of human settlement. Rivers and river valleys belong to all classes of landforms. As has been seen, their valleys and flood plains offer sites for habitation which are the most favored of all. The world population map shows concentrations of population in every valley and on each delta within a favorable latitude. Coastal features often provide sites for concentrations of settlements. Indentures because of tectonic movements, mouths of rivers, coastal features such as off-shore bars and spits, and irregularities in the coast-line—such features provide the sites for harbors and coastal cities and communities. More than likely these features will be found at the outlets of plains regions, so there is a natural routeway into and out of the greater area of settlement. Shorelines of lakes serve a similar function, with the patterns of settlement following the outline of the inland water body. The Great Lakes Region of North America is an outstanding example of this phenomenon of settlement.

Latitude combines with the distribution of landforms to alter the conditions of their use by human settlement. Examples are the mighty rivers flowing to the Arctic Ocean from both North America and the Eurasian continent. They originate in vast plains and wide river valleys. Their drainage basins cannot be densely settled and perhaps never can become important for the numbers of population they can support. The world's landform pattern makes up the physical base for human settlement. However, it cannot be considered separately, because other geographical factors must combine to provide the bases for support of concentrations of human population.

population distribution and climatic types

The world's climatic regions form a very important world pattern affecting the arrangement of population and of man's settled areas. Some climatic regions provide nearly optimum conditions for man's effective use of a region. Certain climatic conditions permit the production of an ample food supply, and there may be other products obtained from the soils and from the land that serve industrial needs or which add convenience for the human inhabitants. Other climatic types have conditions which are restrictive. Living in their areas may be difficult because of unfavorable temperature conditions, either too warm or too cold; or the rainfall regime may be inadequate, either by season or by the year. The set of climatic elements within the locational setting and in combination with the set of land forms and other geographic variables is a pattern which is very closely matched by the distributions of human settlement.

Climatic studies have been made by many scholars for many years. Numerous attempts have been made to classify regions of similarity and differences on a world map and to show their distributions. All of them have in common an effort to show the areas which offer advantages or disadvantages for man. It is not the purpose of this text to review the classifications nor to evaluate them. Instead, it is proposed here that some generally recognized names of a few climatic regions be used and that these serve as illustrations to show the relationship of the world's areas of settlement and the climate pattern.

Four types of climate are particularly well suited to supporting a heavy concentration of human population. First are the *Humid Subtropical* climates with extensive areas in southeastern Asia, southeastern United States, and the eastern side of South America south of the Tropic of Capricorn. These match quite well the densely settled areas in their respective continents. Smaller areas in South Africa, eastern

Australia, and even in southeastern Europe have concentrations of population within their regions of Subtropical Climate. The second climatic type which matches some great areas of settlement is the *Tropical Wet-and-Dry* (or *Savanna*), a warm climate with an extremely heavy rainfall during the summer and relative drouth during the season of low sun. In India, the greatest concentration of population is located within this climatic region. The same climate extends into parts of southeast Asia, and there again the concentrations of population match the savanna lands. The patterns of correspondence are different in Africa, South America, and northern Australia. It seems that in those continents the savannas are not preferred by human settlers. Some of the vast areas of the *Tropical Wet-and-Dry* climate there actually are restrictive, if the evidence of a low population density is accepted.

Two climates have their distributions in the middle latitudes in rather close agreement with the arrangements of population within the European and North American regions. They are the *Humid Continental* and the *Marine West Coast* climates. Both have adequate rainfall over extensive areas so they can support strong programs of mid-latitude agriculture. Both have variability and seasons, and both have rainfall distributed throughout the year even though the maxima and minima are reversed. Summer rainfall characterizes the continental climates of interior Europe and eastern North America; winter rainfall maxima are noted in western Europe with oceanic influence and along the narrow coastal strip of the north Pacific littoral of western North America. Neither climate has a set of temperatures which are restrictive to western man's health or his activity. Instead there are changes which some geographers have pointed out as having contributed to the energetic set of activities which are part of the livelihood of European types of settlement.

The *Mediterranean Climate* is one which is represented on all six continents. In each instance there is a substantial population within the warm to hot, "summer dry-winter wet" area. Chile, South Africa, Australia, and central and southern California have concentrations of population within their restricted areas of this climatic regime. The Mediterranean littoral is extensive. Both the European and the African sides and the western lands of Asia's Middle East have many characteristic nodes of settlement that relate to the unusual type of climate. In aggregate, the Mediterranean climate has many people, although population is so dispersed that it cannot be named as a climatic region having major concentrations of settlement.

population distribution and the resource base

All over the world there must be a basis for support of the human population of the region. This need is supplied by the resource base.

There must be a means of producing a food supply; there must be a supply of raw materials needed for the people to carry on their own livelihood; and men must have means for housing and supporting themselves. This resource base is necessary whatever is the stage of the population's economic development. A part of the pattern of human settlement is the arrangement any community may have to acquire goods by exchange in order to have the variety of products needed for the total pattern of living. The resource base varies greatly from region to region, with some areas especially favored and others very poor indeed.

The resource base has within it a combination of several geographical distributions. The regime of an hospitable climate, land suitable for agriculture, a forest resource, or a set of minerals which may be mined— these serve to illustrate the elements of a strong resource base. If resources are available in sufficient amounts, a region may well support a dense population. There must be opportunity for further development of an economic structure, too, and this the resource base must anticipate.

A population map with its areas of densely settled communities is an evidence of the fortunate combination of several elements of the resource base available to that population group. Also, it shows that the settled area has an organization enabling it to use the natural advantages of its region. Similarly, a vacant or sparsely settled area indicates some shortage of essential ingredients, so the economy lags and development is not a well established system. The lack may be a cultural one, with the population itself failing to make the development which would be possible within the area. Backwardness in some form, poor government, lag in technological development, or inadequate attention to developing systems of exchange may leave some resources unused. Because of some of these reasons the economic structure may not be developed to its potential. A population map is considered as being at the same time a map of the resource base and one of the stage of development of the separate communities. It does not lack much in being a map of the standard of living when comparisons are made of the potential and the developed share of the resource base.

Areas with Sparse Population

Four-fifths of the earth's land surface is sparsely settled. Some areas carry no resident population at all. In total, however, sparsely settled regions have many people. The one-tenth of all the people on earth who live outside of the great concentrations of settlement are widely dispersed. Their communities are very different in form and function from region to region. In general the dispersed settlements show something of the rigors of the area or region where they are located. In some of them the population lives well. Neighbors are not numerous, but the population has a fine adjustment to the resources of the land. Other regions can provide only a marginal living for the few people who remain there, often with only a subsistence type of living. There are even a few extensive areas which have conditions so inhospitable that there is no resident population at all.

Some extensive regions have resources enough for a limited population, fairly evenly distributed but continuing to live in a manner adjusted to the conditions of the community. This form of settlement frequently is adjacent to an area where population is concentrated. Other communities are remote and isolated so that the residents struggle for a living at a subsistence level. Still other settlements may be subsidized outposts of the larger communities, with some form of activity or production that is earning the subsidy. Areas of sparse population may be characterized by widely distributed settlements concentrating the special production of unusually endowed areas so there can be an exchange program set up with the greater communities of the corelands. Or they may be very small settlements, widely distributed and providing marginal living. Again, some world regions still have nomadic peoples who live remotely and plan their living at some higher form than a subsistence level. Finally, many areas are so remote and so inhospitable that the barest living can be made within their rigorous and restrictive environment.

population distribution by continents

All continents have areas with sparse population. There may be mountainous areas, high plains and plateaus, areas of cold or of extreme heat, areas with excessive rainfall and humidity combined with heat, areas of drouth, and areas with tundras or icy landscapes. Some lands which have better potential support for groups of settlers are remote so that contacts with more populous areas are difficult. Many islands and island groups may be included among these sparsely settled areas. There, as within the continental masses, difficulty of making contacts may keep the forms of livelihood extremely rigorous for the people concerned.

Asia has its full share of areas with sparse population, despite the fact of there being nearly two-thirds of the world's people on that continent. The central part of Asia has a very high plateau ringed with systems of the world's highest mountains. These mountain systems seem to divide the continent into huge natural regions. Mountain systems make formidable barriers for the men who wish to travel from one vast area to another. The Plateau of Tibet is within the interior of the continent, a two-mile high plateau enclosed by mountains of far greater height. There are other enclosed areas, the Tarim Basin, the Gobi, and

Sinkiang. Mongolia is a great dry plateau to the east, and other plateau areas extend westward to form the interior of Afghanistan and Iran. Even further west in Asia Minor the Anatolian Plateau provides the highland interior of Turkey.

The interior locations of Asia have one thing in common: dryness. Uplands are cold. Long cold seasons are the rule for the plateaus and the interiors, even in the lower mid-latitudes. Two generations ago, geographers frequently called the extensive middle of the continent the "Dead Heart of Asia." That appellation is not so appropriate today, for transportation routes have given access to the territory and its resources. Some rail lines and roads that carry freight trucks have entered the region from both the Soviet Union and from China's settled communities.

North of the great mountain systems lies the vast territory of Siberia, almost as large as the South American continent. There, too, plateaus are found, and between them are vast lower plains with great river valleys opening toward the Arctic. Boreal forests prevail in regions where the lands and the climate permit. Settled communities occupy areas that are strategic for routeway stations or are at favored places in river valleys where timber stands are processed so that lumber can be sent to the western core areas of the Soviet Union. Other sites for settlement are at the stations where mineral deposits can be worked. Again, the minerals, including gold, platinum, and diamonds, as well as many baser metals, are needed by the populated regions to the west. Outposts line the river outlets to the Arctic Ocean, each one a subsidized community doing its part in a communication system for the country. The largest settlements of Siberia line the routeway of the Trans-Siberian Railway along the southern border of the area, north of the mountainous divide. West of the mountains the routeway follows the strip of arable land north of the interior drouth regions of Central Asia westward to the Urals and beyond. The Turk-Siberian Railroad follows the line of settlements around the southern rim of the Central Asia region, thereby connecting present-day communities which are built on the locations of some of the very oldest settlements of the continent and of the world.

Europe's northern area beyond 60° North is one of sparse settlement. Those lands of Scandinavia, Finland, and northern European Russia have sparse population in comparison with that of most of Europe. Arable land is scarce, the seasons are short for agriculture and horticulture. Much of the land is forested. Besides, there are mineral deposits which are mined, and near their workings are communities which make every effort to be self-supporting. The pattern of settlement is one of an all-over thinly distributed population, with many communities specializing in lumbering, mining, fishing, or maintenance of a port or transportation center.

Europe is the continent which has the smallest proportion of its area unsuited for the use of man. Mountain areas which forbid settlement are very restricted in area. The Iberian Peninsula with a plateau as its dominant feature is at a latitude where human habitation is possible. Settlement there is part of the Mediterranean type, with densely populated centers and restrictive community units alternating with sparsely settled slopes and highlands, some of them being parts of mountain systems. Dryness and a limited supply of arable land place their characteristic pattern on Mediterranean settlement. Also, throughout the region there is an accessibility of each settled area to the sea. The coastline and the climate pattern place their marks on Mediterranean settlements.

Generally speaking, the traditional "Near East" populated areas reflect the adaption of human settlement to one factor: dryness. Border lands of the eastern Mediterranean, including Turkey, Lebanon, Syria, Israel, and Egypt, and the lands farther inland (Anatolia, the Arabian Peninsula, Iraq, and Iran) are in total not densely populated. Everywhere the settlements are of the oasis-type. Even the exotic desert rivers (Nile, Tigris-Euphrates, and Indus) are really a form of oasis. They extend outward as far as land can be made productive by irrigation or by some of modification of the aridity. Settlements there may be found at stations where centuries-old caravan stops formed the foundations of present-day cities. Routeways and the servicing of them have always been a dominating factor in the location of settlements of Mediterranean and Near Eastern lands. The same system of communication lines has extended into Central Asia, into the Indian Subcontinent, and into the heart of Inner Asia. The caravan stop and way-station and its supporting small settlement is a feature of the dry lands of the very central areas of the Eurafasian land mass.

Africa has several features which are distinctive among the continents in their effect on population distribution. Almost all of the continent has hot climates because of its position astride the Equator. The continent is vast with many contrasting sets of conditions, with the world's most extensive desert area, an extensive rain forest region, and much savanna land. Also, a great deal of the continent is dominated by plateaus, some of which have mountain areas upon them. There is a treasure house of minerals in the continent, too, with many great deposits in such size that the world's countries vie with each other for access to them. Small portions of the continent have major concentrations of settlement. However, for the most part the established communities are located where there is a particular resource to exploit, a special product to be produced for the world market, or where there is an advantageous way stop along the world's transport lines. Communities which have been listed as major settlements in the preceding section of this text have centered within the areas which have available arable land.

Africa's rain forests inhibit settlement. At their margins are some large cities. Generally speaking most settlements are small and widely distributed. Savanna lands do not have large settlements in the African setting unless their cities are associated with a mineral production center. Some areas of West Africa have agricultural districts that are devoted to production of crops for export. In them there is considerable dispersal of settlement. Ground nuts (peanuts) grown in northern Nigeria and the palm oils produced nearer the coast of the Gulf of Guinea are examples of such specialization.

Africa turns to advantage the vast part of the continent which is a plateau. Plateaus are favored in this continent, in contrast with those lands in both Eurasia and North America where they are sparsely inhabited even if they are settled at all. Africa's plateau lands are nearer the Equator, where an average elevation of 2,000 to 5,000 feet above sea level provides lowered temperatures than near the coast (3.5° F. per 1000 feet decrease of temperature with altitude). Thus the savanna lands, veld, bush, and sudan are suitable for man who is comfortable in the temperature ranges usually associated with middle latitudes. Some of the agricultural practices of mid-latitudes can be carried on in the higher lands of eastern Africa, with a dispersed settlement in that part of the continent. Mineralized areas of Zambia and Rhodesia and those extending farther south into the Republic of South Africa have nodes of settlement at the location of the mining areas with good sized urban communities as their centers.

Africa's vast Sahara is a physical feature unmatched in size anywhere in the world. Its conditions of heat and lack of water make it one of the earth's most rigorous natural environments. Saharan oases have been traditionally used for centuries as stops for caravans. Their settlements are small in size and in number, perhaps with the balance of available support and the numbers of people as finely drawn as any place in the world. The present exploration for petroleum within the Sahara is an example of a long-practiced program of older established communities building outposts in a remote area. There is a continual search in such locations, trying to find a resource or commodity which is of value to the residents of the world's densely settled regions. In hot regions or cold, wet regions or dry, remote outposts are established to obtain a coveted item. The people concerned who live in remote communities are always aware of the market which is away but on which they must depend.

Australia has a total population of about twelve million people. This is a sparse total population in comparison with that of any other continent. As was shown earlier, Australia's population is along the edge of the continent. The most important concentration of settlement is found in the southeast where extensive inland settled communities radiate away from the great coastal cities which are the largest on the continent. Beyond the basic settled region, the rest of the continent is sparsely settled indeed. Farming and grazing land give way to the inland deserts. Some of these are listed among the world's hottest and driest desert regions. Certainly they are the most extensive dry areas of the southern hemisphere.

Settlements are often isolated and are widely spaced within the interior of Australia. Several of them owe their locations to mineral deposits. The largest concentration of such mining communities is inland from Perth, in Australia's southwest. That city is a port and an outlier of the core area to the southeast. A single cross-continent railroad connects the group of settlements and their rail system to the larger settlements of the eastern coastal region. The whole settlement of the continent is new in comparison with that of all other continents. Its three million square miles of area has a distribution of its minor settlements that is remindful of the oasis nodes in the Middle East.

Despite North America's having one of the major concentrations of the world's population, nearly five-sixths of the continent is sparsely settled. Three important differences are found in an analysis of the distribution of population of North America in comparison with that of other continents which have areas of sparse settlement. First, there is a great concentration of settlement in the western tier of states of the United States and adjacent Canada. Except for the distance between that area and the major regions of population to the east, the settlement's concentration is similar to that of the core area of the continent. Second, there is a great area of widely dispersed settlement, thinly distributed on the farm and ranch lands of the Great Plains region. It has cities of major size, surrounded by an all-over pattern of settlement that is well inter-connected by transportational systems within the region and with other populated areas of the continent. Third, the settlements of the cold areas and of the dry areas are somewhat similar to those of other continents. They have small nuclei or nodes of settlement, often widely set apart, depending upon the region or upon the available supply of resources. Again, the major differences exist because of the better transportation contacts available to them and to the region at large.

North America has a great deal of its area in northern latitudes. Its territory which extends into the *Subarctic* and the *Tundra* climatic regions can have only a few people. The giant river valleys of the Yukon and the MacKenzie Rivers, the Canadian Shield, and the islands of Canada's North have very few people. Most of them are located at strategic outposts where there is a mining development that earns a subsidy from the communities of the core. Alaska's settlement likewise is concentrated in smaller compact communities which are making a serious effort to be self-supporting within the State's area. The cold lands extend southward to meet the sparse settlement of the interior where agriculture and also ranching make possible a thin but widely distributed form of occupance.

The Rocky Mountain Cordillera, extending from Alaska to Mexico, and enclosing several great basins and plateaus, is a mighty structural feature of the North American continent. It has many favored locations for settlement, in mountain enclosed valleys, in its routeways, in passes, and in its basin areas. Settlements near the Great Salt Lake, in the Snake River and the Columbia River valleys, in the Bighorn Basin, and in the plateaus of the American Southwest and Mexico illustrate the communities which the region supports. Facing eastward are several centers between the mountains and the western boundary of the High Plains, such as those of Montana, Wyoming, and Colorado with Denver and Colorado Springs which stand at the gateways to the Middle Rocky Mountain region. Aridity and dryness plague the mountainous area generally so that irrigation of suitable areas forms the basis of support for specialized forms of agriculture. Ranching and stock raising characterize the most extensive use of land in the West. Many communities show by their location the relationship with major mineral deposits which are being worked in the mountainous region.

The areas of sparse population in North America are closely integrated in functional structure with the densely settled areas of the continent. In the Far West the settlements of California, Oregon, and Washington partake somewhat of the oasis-like distribution of other continents. North America's western settlements are extensive; they have an adequate transportation and communication network; and their economy is integrated totally with that of the eastern section of the continent. The transportation system of the east extends to the Great Plains to provide that region with a network adequate to its needs for the agricultural specialization of the area and for the cities that are regional centers and capitals. Mexico's northern area is dry for the most part, with mountain and plateau country extending as far south as the Tropic of Cancer. Communities are small, generally, located as in the Rockies farther north, at strategic way stations and in small, favored valleys. The west coast is too dry and hot for substantial numbers of people. Larger communities and some cities are located along the coast of the Gulf of Mexico south of the Rio Grande River.

Nearly three-fourths of South America's area is sparsely settled despite its location across the Equator. It seems unexpected that, besides heat that is to restrict settlement, both cold and drouth appear to make parts of the continent inhospitable. In general, as has been seen, the concentrations of settlement are near the coast or in areas tributary to coastal outlets. The interior is often underdeveloped with extensive areas inhabited by only a few people. In this continent which may be the world's most rapidly growing human settlement of all (TABLE 2.6), the lands most sought after for human use are restricted in extent.

The *Tropical Rain Forest* has an area in South America even greater in size than in Africa. The Amazon Basin at the heart of the continent, joined with extensive river basins of other drainage systems north and south, includes the forested climatic region and the great savanna areas that flank it on both sides. Those climates are restrictive in South America, as in Africa, and population waits many developments which will make it possible for man to go into the region comfortably. South America's hot-wet and hot wet-dry regions carry a small population.

Cold and drouth are present especially in the Andean region of the western side of South America. The cordillera is a formidable barrier to all communication, and it creates cold climatic conditions because of its elevation. Population is located in favored river valleys, in intermontane basins, and upward along the Andean slopes as high as 10,000 feet or more above sea level. Despite its rigors, many people live in the mountainous areas. Major proportions of the population of Peru, Bolivia, Equador, and Colombia are located in high Andean communities. The spine of the Andes extends southward to 55°, at the southern tip of the continent, providing beyond 40° South an area with very limited settlements of any kind, either within the mountains or on their flanks. Even the narrowing plain of Patagonia, east of the mountains themselves, has almost no permanent settlement.

An extensive dry region is located in northeastern Brazil, restricting settlement in that area. Coastal locations have large cities and communities that extend inland from the populous centers. Generally speaking, however, the dry area restricting inhabitants is adjacent to the savanna and the lower Amazon Basin with low density settlement of central Brazil. Several communities are set up because of mineral deposits in Brazil's interior. Also, in the southern part of the savanna area, well inland from the coastal settlements centering on Rio de Janeiro and Santos, Brazil is building its new capital, Brasília. This is a prelude, perhaps, to an extensive opening up of the interior of the country.

Noteworthy for its intensity within a very limited extent is the dry and desert area west of the Andes along the Pacific Coast. There in southern Peru and northern Chile the Atacama Desert prohibits settlement in all except the centers of nitrate and copper mining where small cities are specialized in production of minerals for export. Across the Andes, the mines of the high, mountainous flanks in Bolivia provide tin and copper in amounts that make this part of the continent important among world producers of these metals. Cities of the region, like those of Columbia to the north, are often centers of mineral production. Already mentioned have been the favored communities of Venezuela at the north end of the continent, with great oil fields and with one of the world's most important deposits of iron ore. Mineral production is a way of life for many settlements in South America.

population distribution by latitudes

Latitude is an element in the distribution of sparse settlement in the world's regions, even as it affects the areas of densely peopled regions. Combined with other elements, some of them also restrictive, the location within the various latitudinal belts offers a partial explanation for the forms of occupance of some world communities. People are settled in certain areas in small numbers, often according to items of location measured in distances from the Equator.

The low latitudes have restricted the size of the human settlements. Near the Equator usually there is not a high density of population. As has been seen, local advantages of the situation, such as the areas that have a plateau-like altitude, provide some favored populous communities in the belt of 10° North to 10° South Latitude. Great urban centers generally avoid the equatorial latitudes. Several coastal positions provide sites for cities of importance on both continental and island locations. Singapore's location as an entrepôt, just north of the Equator where the traffic of the Indies and Southeast Asia converge, is an outstanding exception to the basic patterns of settlement. It is a location established by the world's commercial pattern as well as by a local situation.

Outer low latitudes have population concentrations on the eastern portions of the continental areas, while the western sides are almost uninhabited deserts. In the northern hemisphere, the Sahara and Arabian Deserts, the desert region of the middle East and Pakistan, and the desert areas of the North American Southwest have in common a sparse settlement with small communities in only the exceptionally favored sites. The southern hemisphere has three areas within these latitudes described traditionally as the "trade wind desert latitudes."

They are the small area of the Atacama, the Kalahari, and the Australian deserts. Again, in all three areas, the desert extends to the ocean's coastline. Small settlements only are found in each location.

Just outside the latitude of the great deserts is the location of the Mediterranean climates on the west sides of the continents and the subtropical climates at matching latitudes to the east. The contrast in settlement forms is extreme, as has been described above, for these outer limits of the low latitudes and for the equatorward sides of the middle latitudes. The dryness of the western areas during long high-sun seasons contrasts with the humid long-summer climates of the eastern regions to be more effective as population controls than the latitude factor alone.

Middle latitudes have been shown as those dominated chiefly by westernized settlement. Continental interiors with dry areas are chief restrictors of dense populations in these latitudes. The interior of North America has a light population density west and north of the core area of the continent's settlement. In Asia, China is exerting every effort to bring the drier interior lands into production of some kind to contribute to the food supply for the country. China's core settlement belongs to the subtropics; North America's and Europe's basic settlements are in the middle latitudes.

High latitudes are restrictive for settlement in both of the continental masses which encircle the Arctic Ocean. Small settlements are found within Alaska and northern Canada where a functional advantage is to be noted: a mining area, a fishing community, or an airbase. Outposts are located in northern Europe and Siberia, again with mining centers or as termini for short railroads processing and shipping lumber, as ports, as strategic outposts for the Northern Sea Route, or as airbases. Some small centers of settlements in the high latitudes are chiefly established as service areas for the regions.

Basic Features of Human Settlement

The most important feature of human settlement is its uneven distribution over the earth's land area. The major proportion of the population is concentrated in those areas which offer physical advantages for human use. These advantages are tied often to the availability of arable land and to a climatic regime which provides growing conditions for food crops in adequate supply for the heavy need. The pattern of the world's land forms provides the setting for its population concentrations. Also, it makes most areas restrictive, for there is not arable land enough for further development at the stage of technology of the inhabitants of the given region.

Both the world's densely settled regions and those of sparse settlement are significant for a population study. Built into the patterns are the supplies of the world's resources and the installations man has made to use them. Mineral deposits to provide needed metals and the fuel and power sources may or may not be used to advantage. This reflects itself in the occupational structure, in every form of structure of the settlements, and ultimately in the standard of living of the people within the areas of settlement. Transportational media are represented in the patterns of settlement. For example, concentrations of settlement along coasts, in valleys which may or may not have water transportation, or at breaks in transportation, all these and others affect the livelihood of the population and the manner of living within the communities. The adequacy of the interregional transportational system is a strong influence on the overall settlement pattern.

As outlined in the beginning of this chapter, there is often a close relationship apparent within the distributions of human settlement and the earth's physical features. This has been established in a general way in a review continent by continent and region by region. It is well not to lose sight of the differences between the "expected" or the "logical" correspondence of the patterns and the way they truly exist. Differences in peoples, and in population groups, in their states of technology, and in their degree of effort to achieve a better way of living in a given circumstance all alter the basic geographical patterns. Some groups are already anticipating and planning for more intensive and more effective use of their supply of the world's resources. Others are not aware of that need and are doing little to forestall more difficulties which will arise with an ever-growing population.

Chapter **4**

Cultural Bases of Human Settlement

Many elements of cultural geography are woven into the patterns of human settlement. Human institutions and man-made features dominate almost every landscape. Most of them are material in their nature, indicating forms of endeavor which allow people of a cultural group to make use of a region and its physical assets. In some areas the cultural heritage may be manifest in the patterns of today. Evidences of long historical precedent, of basic philosophies, of tradition appear on the landscape. In contrast, sometimes the most apparent patterns may reflect changes from a former system of occupance; even an innovation may be made by the present cultural group in a setting formerly used very differently. Then, too, there are regions which reflect the very newness of their human settlement. A population group with its cultural pattern already set recently may have entered the new area bringing a particularly advanced form of settlement to the pioneer community. The cultural landscape is a record of the background of the population in the region. It records with its features many facets of the lives and backgrounds of the peoples concerned. In the structure of the present settlement is a record of the activities and the living of the population of today.

Besides the numbers of people and their distribution on a population map there are many geographical patterns which give meaning to the world's human settlement. The most prominent pattern is that of the world's political units. Most often noted is the distribution of the nations, countries, and territories by the political map. Within that basic outline, there is added meaning for the maps of the world's peoples showing nationality, languages, and religions. Also noted is the fact that there are important records for human settlement in the occupational structure of the regions and countries of the world. These patterns show the forms of livelihood and the stages of economic development of the communities concerned. They can show something of the degree of industrialization, the incomes, and the use of the sets of natural resources. Also, an analysis of the cultural bases of settlement becomes almost individualized. Income, national and per capita; food consumption and dietary patterns; health and life expectancy; and literacy all apply to individuals within the world society. The distribution of countries, of peoples, and of their cultural relationships in regional settings is a critical record of human settlement.

Political Patterns of World Settlement

The political map is a record of nationality of population groups and the areas which they occupy. It is presently a very complex pattern, drawing upon thousands of experiences and relationships among peoples of the past and of the present in an effort to establish for every individual a basis for his own sense of belongingness and allegiance. For the individual and for his fellows there is offered a sense of loyalty, of patriotic concern, and of nationality. Nationals of a country think of their own people, their own area, their resources and facilities, and of their boundaries. They think of their relationships with other sets of people, of their contacts, of kinships, of rivalries, of interests in treaties and trade, and of agression or defense. Everyone's country is his homeland to be loved, supported, and given his pledge of support. The political map identifies the units of human settlement.

There are about 130 sovereign states in the world and many more countries which are separate entities, although politically associated with other nations. Each one has a government, whether the country be large or small, fully independent or dependent. There are several giant countries which occupy more than three million square miles: Soviet Union, Canada, China, United States, and Brazil. Australia with Tasmania barely misses that size. Other countries are of much less area, even though they may have very large populations. India, with an area one-third that of the United States, now has a population of more than 450 million people. Land areas of other countries range downward to only a few square miles. Their sizes in some instances may be measured in acres. Population sizes vary also, ranging from hundreds of millions of people downward to the size that matches the numbers of people in a middle-sized city or town.

Every country has its own identity and its own population within a definite spatial area. Each has its nationality and its government which acts for its people. That government represents its people as it deals externally with other countries and domestically with the economic structure of its own community. Currently as this study is being prepared, there are 122 members of the United Nations. Also, a tradi-

tional and longstanding organization of countries, the British Common-
wealth, has 22 members. There are political groupings among nations;
as, NATO, SEATO, the Arab League, and the "Communist Bloc." Each
group carries out meaningful dealings among its members and with
other groups or countries. Thus they serve the roles of extra-sized political units.

A political map for the geographer is a master index of the world's
countries. Details of size of area, boundary delimitation, location, re-
cordings of data of every kind, naming of peoples according to their
nationality, ethnic stock, or allegiance, and all kinds of international
relationships are presented on the world political map. The reader is
encouraged to use an atlas as he reads this and later chapters.

Cultural Patterns of Settlement

Evolution and growth of man's cultural patterns have resulted from
thousands of years of civilization's development. The record of the past
has projected meaning into the distributions of settlement today. Cultural inclinations and distributions are the patterns of human life itself.
They include descriptions and groupings of peoples in a physical sense
and define them by their sets of beliefs, loyalties, group attitudes, efforts,
and group relationships.

Many areal maps have been prepared to show the distribution of
the world's peoples and their cultural heritage. Some of them show
world patterns, while others give details for smaller areas. Together
they present the structural framework for human settlement. Although
many patterns could be used, the present study is using three to
depict the record of human differences in the world. Maps of racial
stock, languages, and religions reveal a great deal of man's past and
his origins. These patterns have come out of the long-distant past, prehistoric and historic. They show something of common ancestry, common areas of origin, and of population migrations long ago and recent.
They show man's differences and the reflection of differing settings
as places of origin for his many racial stocks and for his cultural beginnings.

Racial and cultural groupings are the bases for human existence in
civilized population groups. Distributions are changing today more
rapidly than ever before. Population growth overall is accelerating, as
was shown in preceding chapters; and more readily achieved intercommunication of peoples is the present mode. Race, language, and
religion, although they evolved during a very long period of time,
are certainly changing. And they are changing more rapidly than at
any time in history. Intercommunication and intermingling of peoples
alter the structures of the patterns within themselves as well as trans-
posing them from area to area and from region to region.

racial and ethnic patterns of settlement

There are great differences in the physical appearance and major characteristics of different population groups over the world. From time immemorial, men have attempted to classify their own kind into "races." They have noted features of similarity and of contrast and have attempted to devise a form of classification that would give appropriate names to groups of people in different regions. Efforts at naming and describing peoples have been attempted by every human group. Even so, no system has been entirely satisfactory because the variety of people is so large. Perhaps there will never be a generally accepted set of descriptive names for *homo sapiens*, the genus and species to which all living men belong.

The mixing of groups of population in the past has created many "in-between" peoples. Some of those groups have been named, with the acceptance of those names making additions to the lists for the general classifications. The distribution of those new peoples preserves a record of past migrations, captivities, alliances, interbreeding, and differential population growth.

Differing characteristics of peoples tell much of the ethnic history of various peoples. The population pattern of today is a record of human settlement and its dispersal from the foci of origin of major cultural groups. A map of the "Races of the World" is a record of present-day population distributions, while at the same time it presents the patterns of growth and extension of settlement from the earliest to the most recent times.

Distribution of the world's peoples within the major continental divisions demonstrates some very significant features of the settlement as the pattern of races is analyzed. The major points of the general distributions are observed and tabulated as follows:

1. Mongoloid peoples have inhabited most of the eastern half of Asia, with their numbers constituting one-third of the population of the earth. It is significant to note that the native peoples of the Americas, those of eastern Siberia, and part of those of the East Indies are classified as this racial stock.

2. Africa south of the Sahara was the original home of Congoid peoples, the only continental area with that racial stock. An enclave of Capoid people was located in southern Africa between the Cape and Kalihari regions. The numbers of this stock make up about seven percent of the world population today.

3. Australoid peoples were the original stock of Australia and the eastern part of the East Indies. Interestingly, there is shown on the map some small areas of settlement in India and Japan

where members of a similar population were found among the original settlers of the regions.

4. The widespread distribution of the Caucasoid people is a marked feature of the map. From the original homeland, believed to be within the Middle East and the Caucasus mountain and plateau region, it extended eastward into most of the Indian Sub-Continent, westward across the northern part of Africa, north and westward into all of Europe, besides Russia and part of Siberia. This stock may be characterized as "Western" peoples as distinguished from the Orientals farther east on the great continental land area. These people constitute more than half of the total world population.

5. Transplanted Caucasoid peoples are a marked feature of the world map. In the Americas, they submerged the indigenous Mongoloid peoples, the tribal groups of the American Indians, so that today those peoples of the original stock are almost enclaves within the major settlement pattern of their own continent. In Australia and New Zealand there was the same record of encroaching settlement, usurping the land of the Bushmen and the Maoris.

   The Caucasoids merged with other stocks with which they came into contact, so that in all, as the map shows, their numbers including such amalgamated peoples number now more than half of the world's inhabitants. This widespread distribution of "Western people" beyond their original location is the most striking feature of their settlement. They occupy about one-third of the world's land area.

The map of the world's racial groups demonstrates that population groups have behaved differently as their numbers have increased within their original regions. The strength of some stocks has been that they have continued to dominate their original areas. Other groups, particularly the Caucasoids, appear to have been continually moving. Regions of their conquest and colonization have extended far beyond their place of origin. They have mixed with indigenous peoples of every continent, have replaced many less numerous groups, and have set their stamp on the structure of settlement in all of those regions. TABLES 2.3 and 2.4 in Chapter 2 of this study present their numbers within "Areas of European Settlement." By a sharp contrast, the Mongoloid peoples still residing in their continent of origin, hold to their own identity, and to a great extent their own cultural patterns despite the contacts with agressive colonizing Westerners.

It is important to remain aware that there is no satisfactory index for identifying and classifying groups of human population. For example, the traditional concept that Europeans are light-skinned people disappears when one notes that Caucasoid peoples include many groups that have very dark pigmentation. Certainly, various population groups have differing characteristics within their physical makeup. There are even more variations in the forms of their cultural expressions. One can observe that there are separate characteristic behavior patterns which are followed by the descendants of the original inhabitants of the world's major land areas. These differences are evident in the cultural patterns of settlement.

language patterns in settlement

Distribution of languages and language families is a major cultural pattern. The world map of today's languages supports the historical record of peoples within their home regions, where they were sedentary long enough to develop their own patterns of oral and written communication. The language map shows evidences of the migrations of long ago and the fusing of ancient human stocks. The record is much better understood when considering the changes and growth within the past 500 years. Changes within that time period have been rapid because migrations during the Age of Discoveries made many alterations in the total patterns of peoples distribution and their cultural attributes. Languages are perhaps the greatest gifts of man's cultural heritage. Language distributions of today record many ties with historic and even prehistoric distributions of population groups.

Patterns of world language vary significantly from those of race. Language families, speech patterns related by origin to areas, and similarities in syntax and word meanings show a great deal of persistence for individual world regions. Language patterns have tended to persist in their areas even while they have divided, subdivided, and evolved within restrictive communities. Sub-families of languages are many, and variations and dialects within those sub-families are myriad. It has proven impossible to record all of the variants of languages on a world map. A map of large scale for a particular area, even one for a single country, poses a great problem in presenting the detail needed. For example, a map of the Indian Subcontinent would be required to show some 200 separate languages. In North America, where transplanted Indo-European languages dominate, the map legend for all language groups would be very long if ancestral languages of the American Indians' tribal families were plotted. Many Indian languages remain in use today. A map of languages can only present a generalized distribution of this basic cultural pattern.

There are many coincident features in the patterns of languages and those of the original home of ethnic groups. This is a marked feature in the settlement of the Old World. The greatest area of all in which this similarity is noted is in eastern Asia. That region, with one-third of the world's peoples, has approximately the same proportion of its residents using languages of the continent: Sino-Tibetan, Japanese, Korean, and other east Asiatic languages. Until now these language areas have not extended far beyond their original regions. As has already been shown, it was not the trend of the Asiatics to become colonizers and take their languages to vast overseas territories. During the Age of Discoveries they began only limited migrations from their home regions. Earlier there was some extension, with the populations and their speech usages moving southward. The Chinese language extended all the way into the East Indies. Modern times have made this language extension even more rapid as Oriental traders moved southward from their homeland into thinly populated areas and virgin territories.

The African continent has continued to carry the languages of its indigenous peoples just as it has carried the population of Congoid and Capoid stock. A multitude of languages dominates the south-Saharan border and the region extending southward to the tip of Africa. Languages of Africa were unwritten for a very long time. Written records were devised after outsiders invaded the continent. Perhaps they were so fragmented because they remained so long as oral languages. It is most remarkable that they have been so virile and have held their own identities despite the pressure of immigrant groups.

Though few in numbers, the peoples of the East Indies and the Australoids developed languages of their own. As with the African peoples, those languages were almost unwritten before the Age of Discoveries brought visitors and foreign settlers. The Papuan and Australian languages and those of the Malayo-Polynesian family had a definite world region. They extended over a vast territory of land and ocean, with the vast distances and the isolation providing the occasion for their independent development.

The extension of Indo-European languages to so many parts of the world is the most prominent feature of the world's language map. Languages of Europe bear common origin with an ancient language believed to have originated in northern India. From that region the language went with the people and the settlement, apparently, to the north and northwest. Beginning its migration in very ancient times it grew so that it encompassed all of Europe. Within the European setting the original language was fragmented. There, different physical boundaries provided communities the degree of isolation needed for separate languages to develop. Mountain systems divided the area, fertile basins or river valleys, peninsulas and islands; all restricted the movement of population groups so that languages crystallized into persistant patterns. Many sub-families of language developed in the home region of the Indo-Europeans, and hundreds of dialects developed,

too. Some of them survived and were disseminated far beyond their
initial regions. When the European people led the great migration
abroad, their language areas extended also. A present-day map shows
half of the world's people speaking variations of an ancient language
from the regional hearth of south Asia in the Indian Subcontinent.

A second large language group was a migrant also, the Semito-
Hamitic family which extended over a vast territorial area. It is the
language of most of North America, East Africa, and the Arabian Peninsula. Because of the dryness of much of the region the population is
sparse so the total numbers of people speaking these languages is not
great in comparison with other users of the great families of speech.
About four percent of the world's peoples use Semito-Hamitic languages.
The language has migrated southward into central Africa and even
in some numbers into southern Africa as well as eastward into India
and Pakistan. Generally, within the basic region extending westward
from Arabia to the Atlantic Ocean, the users of the language are members of the Moslem religious faith.

Vast areas of interior Asia are the regions of the Ural-Altaic language family. The population using these languages do not comprise
a large total number because the region is either too cold, too dry,
or too mountainous for a high density settlement. The world map shows
a wedge of the major Slavic language, Russian, which has entered
Siberia from the west, with its extent generally marking the concentration of Russian settlement east of the Urals.

Enclaves of language families are found in many locations, areas
of varying sizes, of the Old World. The Telugu and Tamil language
area of southern India is an example. The Magyar (Hungarian) language is used by a people who have lived for a long time in an enclosed plains area that is a part of the Danube Valley. There are too
many such enclaves to review in this study. Some of them persist in
very small territorial areas. Another example is the Basque language
of the western Pyrenees and adjacent lowlands of France and Spain.
It differs entirely from the Indo-European languages of its neighboring
districts.

Languages of the Indo-European family group, evolving in a region
extending from northern India to the western peninsulas of Europe,
went with the colonizers from the European home base. Particularly
in the New World, the languages of the invaders became dominant
in both continents. English dominates north of the Rio Grande, with
a French-speaking enclave of settlement that occupies part of the St.
Lawrence Valley and Quebec Province. Some indigenous American
Indian and Eskimo tribes, each speaking its own language, remain
in the north. Several American Indian tribal groups maintain their own
languages within their own communities which are widely spaced

over the United States and Canada. Their numbers are not large, and the tribal languages are badly submerged by the pressure of their neighbors.

English gives way to another set of transplanted Indo-European languages at the Rio Grande River. "Latin America" means that Spanish, Portuguese, and French languages serve the great region. Emigrants use them, and they are elements which have taken over as the communication media even for indigenous peoples of Middle and South America. Portuguese is the language of Brazil while most of the remainder of Latin America uses Spanish as the common language. Enclaves of Indian population remain, using their native languages. They are more numerous than the North American Indian tribal families. Both Americas are a testimony to the European colonization program. An interesting evidence of the past is shown with small enclaved areas. The use of the Dutch language in present-day Surinan, between communities which use French and English, respectively, in French Guiana (French) and Guyana (English), records European settlement along South America's northern coast.

English appears again as a dominating language in Australia and New Zealand and in South Africa. In the first instance, it has almost entirely supplanted the native languages. In South Africa, there is besides the English speaking people a strong element of Afrikaans, a reminder of the early Dutch settlement of the area. Two strong European-originated population groups live in the same area, bringing two separate languages to the region and substituting them for the original languages of the native peoples.

Movements of peoples as colonizers, as colonists, as missionaries, and as traders have carried languages far from their places of origin. The world map of languages shows a strong contrast between peoples who migrated extensively and those who stayed in their own regions. Migrations have become more important during recent decades than at any time in the past. There is need today among all peoples for a *lingua franca*. To some degree there is such a movement in progress with several languages crossing many regional nationality borders. An example is the use of Swahili in eastern Africa. Also in that same region the Hindi language has been retained by the Indian settlers and business people. Elsewhere, Chinese merchants and traders have taken their own speech with their trading occupation to add another language to southeastern Asia and the East Indies. Language, business methods, and settlers have been added to the southern region.

English has had a long history of usage away from its homeland. The past century has seen a great gain in the use of English as the language of commerce. The record of the British colonial empire and its trading policies is strongly set on the world's language map. English has become a "second language" of many countries and regions.

The world needs a common language. Imposing a substitute or a secondary language on any population group is extremely difficult and an all but impossible effort. The learning of a new language is tiresome and time-consuming, and other things are at issue. It is an affront to one's pride and to his feeling of nationality to require him to use other than his mother tongue. Trying to hasten the process of creating or adopting any one language universally could not be accomplished arbitrarily. The problem is complex for one to learn completely how to use a new language; to speak, write, read, and think in the new pattern. It is no wonder that a movement toward use of a *lingua franca* moves so slowly. Yet, there is progress. The United Nations publishes data in several languages, favoring French which is used with English in many dual-language publications. Like English, that language had a wide distribution within the usage of the colonial administrations of France when they had a vast overseas territory. Finding a language on which the world can agree is impossible. The *lingua franca* of the future has several present-day nominations, those coming from Western Europe, Russia, India, and Eastern Asia.

religions in the pattern of settlement

A third map of the world patterns, that of world religions, has many features of its distributions which resemble those of world racial stocks and of world languages. The map of religions is like the others in that it presents major religions as generalized world patterns, although it is simpler in its details. A similarity remains, too, in that the map generalizes an extremely complex cultural pattern.

Within the areas designated for each of the great world faiths there are many differences. Hundreds of variants exist for the major faiths, and many more individual sects characterize each religious family. Everywhere there are small areas which do not conform to the generalization mapped for regions of religious preference. A detailed map of religions is so complex that this world map is unable to show other than major regions. There is a mixing of religions within almost any region which can be mapped, for boundaries between regions cannot be closely defined. The distribution of religions and their evidences in human settlement are important elements of the geographic landscape.

Many evidences of the religious preferences of the world's peoples are shown in the patterns of settlement. Much of the history of the area is shown by the buildings and other landscape features associated with the devotional life of the community. Besides, just as mosques, temples, cathedrals, and churches are prominent features in each settlement, there is a geographic imprint left on each area because of religious practices and observances. A great deal of the record of population growth which has extended from basal communities, of migrations and of colonizations, is related to the religions dominating world regions. There is a record also of captivities, of conquests, and of proselyting converts while settlements were being extended. In truth, "Religion has traveled as the lightest of baggage." It has not always been extended into new regions peaceably nor without serious incident. Religious wars have been perhaps the bloodiest of all. These wars have had long-lasting effects on the distributions of religions on present-day maps. It is of special significance to note that, perhaps even more than for race and language, the patterns of religions transcend present-day political boundaries and those marking the religious preferences of population groups.

The map of the world's religions shows cultural expression in its highest form, with the evidences within the settlement pattern related to the personal elements evident within the setting. Man's temples are the crowning architectural features of each community. His settlement includes basic features in the distribution of land, of roads and street patterns, and of arrangement of the local landscape. Within his planning, the place of worship is given a prominent place. The pattern of settlement records for each member of the community something of his respect for his deity, his spiritual leader, his personal philosophy, and the place of religion in his life.

The map of the world's religions has features in its major distributions which are most significant as elements of the world settlement pattern. A summarization which describes some of the major forms in the distribution of those religions is as follows:

1. The Orient has fostered several great world religions. Probably the Buddhists of China and nearby regions are the most numerous of any one religious faith. Other religions of the region (which comprises Japan, Southeast Asia, and part of Inner Asia) include Shintoism, Confucianism, Lamaism, and several others. They have extended over a vast region as population has grown and as internal migrations have filled the area with settlers.

2. Hinduism is the religion of India. Within the Indian Subcontinent the boundary of the religious preference matches fairly closely the boundaries between India and Pakistan. Their faith has traveled with the Indians. Large numbers of Hindus have settled among the peoples of east and southern Africa. Also, migrants have moved to the New World in important numbers.

3. The Moslem faith was founded in Arabia and has spread widely from that "cradle of religions" which also produced Judaism and

Christianity within the same general region. This faith has spread very rapidly within a few centuries so that now it occupies a vast territory. North Africa, with almost all of the Sahara Desert region included, the East African Horn, Arabia, Anatolia, the heartland of Inner Asia, the Indus River Valley together with Iran and Afghanistan and Malaysia-Indonesia—all these regions are Islamic settlements.

Traditionally it has been accepted that the Moslems have occupied the drier and more sparsely populated regions. The world map shows some significant exceptions. Part of the delta of the Ganges and Bramaputra Rivers, East Pakistan, is dominantly Moslem. There is a predominance of Moslems in Malaysia and Indonesia, areas where wet tropical climates prevail.

There are two distinct divisions of Islamic peoples. Members of the Shiah faith live in Iran and part of Iraq. The Sunni group is more widespread, with adherents distributed as far west as the Atlantic coast of Africa and as far east as Celebes Island.

4. The Christian religion became the faith of Europeans, and it was extended by them as a transplanted faith for peoples in every continent. It is a faith which is widespread today; and even more than the language pattern, it marks the areas where European emigrants went to dominate the settlements away from the home continent. Europeans were militant missionaries.

As with the Moslems who have two strong elements in their religion, there are major divisions among Christians. The three major divisions are represented within the European setting. Roman Catholics dominate western, central, and southern Europe. Protestants are the most numerous element in North Europe, while the Eastern Rites churches are found in the Balkans and much of the more populous parts of the Soviet Union.

Both the Roman Catholic and the Protestant faiths accompanied European settlers to the New World. Latin America is almost entirely Catholic, while North America is generally Protestant. Strong elements of Roman Catholics are found throughout the area, particularly within the urbanized communities. There is a very important region of Roman Catholics in Quebec Province in the enclave of French-speaking Canadians. The Philippine Islanders are Roman Catholic, a heritage of the Spanish colonization of that island group. South Africa, Australia, and New Zealand are Protestant, evidences of European settlement mostly from English and Dutch origin. The Dutch took their religion to distant parts of the East Indies.

Enclaves are noted within several regions. A most remarkable one is the Coptic Christian religion of Ethiopia near the Eastern

Horn of Africa. It has been Christian for many centuries, although it is surrounded by Moslem communities.

5. Judaism is mapped differently from other major religions. Only Israel is mapped by shading, while symbols represent the major concentrations in Europe, the Soviet Union, North Africa, and both Americas. Generally the symbols match the locations of great world cities which are located in the countries of dominantly Christian faiths.

6. A simple world map can hardly be fair to the adherents of other religions whose numbers are small or whose religions are less well known. They have been grouped as "Tribal and Shamanistic Religions." That mapping device conceals the true pattern of hundreds of religions. They vary a great deal from each other and from those better known faiths that number their memberships in millions.

The major distribution of areas with these religions show them to be in remote areas; remote from the concentrated settlements of the westernized world and remote from those areas which had easy access routes for Europeans or for the emigrants who would have brought the Moslem faith. Lands around the Arctic Ocean in the Old and the New World, Central Africa, inner Australia, the most inaccessible areas of the East Indies, and remote fastnesses of the Amazon Basin are mapped with this shading. They are regions which are extensive enough to be shown. Many more separate sects could be mapped if the scale of the map permitted.

Every individual in the world is included in the pattern of the world's religions. Just as religion is a personal value for every person, so is it a part of the cultural pattern of each group of people, in large or small numbers. Religion always is a part of the highest set of values of the individual or the community, large or small. It is a cultural pattern derived from the past, and it is very much woven into the livelihood and the physical structure of any settlement. Intangible though they may seem, near-personal elements are important in affecting the features of the landscape. The group code of living, ideas of the deity, reverence for man's gods, and respect for man's spiritual leaders are examples. Religion affects the way of life, whether it be one's personal philosophy or a highly organized set of observances which may be evident in structural features of the landscape.

Influences on the world's religions are important elements in the livelihood of the earth's people. Legal codes of each country conform to the predominant religion of the area. Many food habits, food taboos, and food preferences are rooted in the religions practiced by the people of the region. Thus there are patterns of trade and exchange of commodities, combinations of trading neighbors and rivals that evolve from religious interests. Natural partners for political agreements and treaties are set within the mapped areas of religions. Personal relationships, such as dress, living habits, and family organization, are rooted in the religion of the family and its members. This important cultural pattern is within the consideration of every phase of human settlement, whether the elements are economic, political, or personal.

Human Settlement and the Resource Base

Man's development of the world resource base reflects the cultural heritage which has directed the form of his activity within the natural setting. The physical area provides a varying combination of natural resources available to man (reviewed in Chapter 3). Cultural bases (described partially in the section just above) are significant because they frequently show some prior inclinations of human population groups to utilize those resources which are offered. The element of time is important: time during which a population group has been numerous enough, enlightened enough, well enough governed, strong enough, and well enough endowed by capital to work together constructively and in concert. The population must be mindful of the advantages to be gained by creative efforts at developing the resource base at hand.

There can be no direct cause and effect between the elements of the resource base and the use man will make of a given set of geographic advantages. The supply of natural resources, even the land itself, cannot dictate man's use. The physical setting can be restrictive, however, making it nearly impossible or unprofitable for man to outline or to follow some specific forms of livelihood in certain areas. The regions with severe restrictions for man's effort were named in Chapter 3. The development of an economic region is by a decision which man must make within his cultural organization. Sometimes the price is too high, and a vast region is undeveloped because the stage of cultural organization or direction is not yet mature enough for the potential of the area to be realized. Other regions are highly developed because the patterns of human culture are mature.

Regions in almost every stage and variety of economic and cultural development appear on the world map. For a generation or so there has been a series of terms used to describe countries and areas that differ from others in the use they are making of their sets of natural resources. Terms used early to describe these economic efforts were "developed" and "undeveloped" nations. These proved to be unsatisfactory terms when it was noted that they were static in meaning. Lately there has come to be wide use of more dynamic terms, such as "developing" and "developed" nations, or "underdeveloped" and "highly developed" nations or regions. The later terminology more nearly represents the efforts of the world's settled areas to increase their own potential and to have their economic growth match that of their population and expanded settlements.

It is along the line of the latter form of analysis that two geographers, Spencer and Thomas, have prepared a map which shows for the world a "Comparative Cultural Development of Earth Resources." Their map is included as Figure 4.1 of this chapter. The world's regions are shown in five categories ranked according to the use of the set of resources and according to the technology employed and the longer-run potentials for the areas concerned. The map links population, population effort, resource base, and stages of development and accomplishment. It states well the growth potential of regions as they attempt to further their progress toward a better living standard for their human population.

The most noteworthy features of Figure 4.1 are the generalizations which it presents for great world regions. The map demonstrates emphatically that there are differences among regions with great populations and those which are highly developed. World regions which have been settled by European stock generally rank high in the classification. The "High Level" category shows western Europe, Anglo-America, and Australia and New Zealand, all regions where westernized culture predominates. Japan is the exception. Still completely Oriental in its population, the economic structure matches that of the other communities who have the highest ranking on the map scale. The industrial program and high technological development of these major regions make them outstanding.

As a record for cultural development of regions, the second category of "Progressive Development" is one of the most interesting of all. The mapped area includes India with its vast population, much of Latin America, some of South Africa, the Mediterranean borderlands, and parts of the Philippines, Malaya, and Sumatra. Spain is in this category along with the Balkans, Mesopotamia and the Near East, and the entire extent of the Soviet Union. In all these regions a great deal of progress has been accomplished during comparatively recent decades.

Regions which are mapped with the symbol for "Advancement Initiated" are located in three continents. Most of the area of China is shown in this third category. Iran is completely included because of its intensive effort within the most recent three decades. Part of the plateau area of eastern and central Africa, South America's interior of Amazonia and its borders, and some of the Central American countries are shown as communities making an effort to develop their own technological potential.

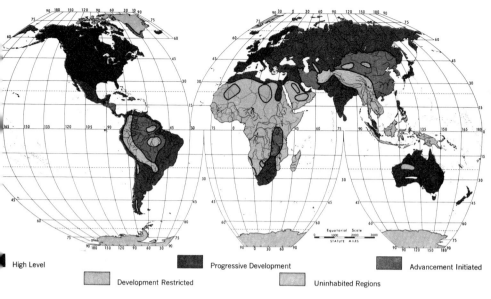

High Level Progressive Development Advancement Initiated

Development Restricted Uninhabited Regions

FIGURE 4.1. Comparative Cultural Development of Earth Resources
(Technology, resources, organization and perception of environmental possibilities.)

Source: J. E. Spencer and William L. Thomas, *Cultural Geography* (New York: John Wiley and Sons, Inc., 1969), p. 370. (Used by permission of the publisher.)

The fourth mapped category, "Development Restricted," makes up a surprisingly large area of the world map. Most of the African continent is included, and there is a restricted area in the Andean region of South America. The mountain core of Asia and the mountainous region extending southeastward to the tip of the continent are shown as other regions with restricted development. Inaccessibility and remoteness are factors restricting the development of the East Indies. Those islands are grouped generally as needing encouragement and help with their future development.

Development of the resource base is a responsibility of the entire world settlement. Technological improvement is necessary and it is certain to come within immediate future time. It is inevitable, for all countries must face further population growth, and the cultural organization must keep pace. Actually, new developments must gain enough to provide a better living everywhere. There particularly is a need in the vast regions where advancement has been slow in developing, as Figure 4.1 shows, so that better opportunities will exist for individual persons as well as for the population groups to which they belong.

Occupational Patterns of Settlement

The basic problem of all human settlement is support for its population. Support comes from use of the land itself and use of the other resources, such as the mineral supply, the forests and the waters of the land, and the products of the ocean. There must be among the world's peoples those who work within a set of occupations that are to convert raw resources to commodities which our cultural organization needs. An economic structure results, world-wide in extent, within which are primary, secondary, and tertiary levels of occupations; all are important for the provision of the livelihood and the living for human settlement. Few regions are completely developed to make full use of their potential, as the foregoing section and Figure 4.1 have demonstrated. It is apparent that there are differences in the stages of development as well as differences for the resource base.

Two basic occupational groups are more important and more basic to the cultural development than others. The first is a primary occupation, the agriculturalist who must make the land provide the food supply. Another group is secondary in nature; its membership is engaged in manufactural and industrial employment. This category is an end product of a highly organized social and economic system. Manufacturing must supply the millions of products which organized society needs and uses. Related to it, of course, are dozens of other occupations such as mining, construction, transportation, trade and commerce, and many others including financial, professional, and governmental workers; each is doing his own part in the complex organizational structure of the economy. It is important to recognize the full set of occupational groups and their contributions while more carefully exploring the two basic occupations which are the mainstays of the economic structure.

sequent occupance

Uses of the land have been named traditionally as the stages in "sequent occupance." There have been stages in the development of the landscape, with the dominant form of livelihood changing in time as the settlement found a new form of activity for the area. The development has not been a regular sequence for the world regions nor has it occurred predictably in time for different areas. Settlement has been made by a complex set of different occupational forms. Not every region has had the same sequence. Sometimes the stages of development have resulted from the varying sets of physical advantages or natural reserves of a resource available for man's use. At other times the background of the human population has set the form of the occupance. The result is a pattern of world settlement which has used, and is presently using, the world's area by a pattern of differing economies which support the world's peoples.

Sequent occupance began with the simplest form of activity, food gathering and hunting, an occupation which developed even in Neolithic times into primitive agriculture. Life was simple, and numbers of people were small. Animal husbandry came in parts of the Old World, and established settlements flourished as people became more numerous. There was not a dropping out of basic occupations as new ones were developed within each region. Instead, there came to be a set of extractive industries which contributed to the better living of the entire group. Sequent occupance provided mining, lumbering, fishing, and trading, all of whose production was needed for the expanding settlement on the land. Communities grew and prospered where there were particularly valuable deposits of minerals or where forest stands were especially abundant and accessible to lumber users in growing concentrations of settlement.

Primitive agriculture became specialized agriculture as the settlement matured, with better ways of using the land developing as markets for the products appeared. Nodes of settlement grew, utilizing the foodstuffs provided to them and serving as a market for the production of extractive occupations that was ready to serve their needs. Urbanization developed as numbers of population increased and as the complexity of the settlement provided more occupations. Meanwhile, the agriculturalists, the pastoralists, the lumbermen, the fishermen, the miners, and others contributed their productivity to building the complex settlement.

There has been from the very earliest stages of settlement an important form of manufactural industry. The modern industrial urban complex is highly organized in production of items which are of value for the well-being of many people. The large community can specialize even as the small population group of long ago could have a member whose contribution was the manufacture of a tool, an article of clothing, or something else which provided for another man's basic needs of food, clothing, and shelter. As geographers have worked out the stages of sequent occupance, it has been realized that the manufactural or industrial stage is the highest form of organization for human settlement. Efficiency of organization is possible within the other forms of occupance also. Agriculture in the greater view differs from region to region. In some instances it is as highly organized as the manufactural plants. In other regions the form is so simple that it resembles the earliest stages of the occupational sequence. It is this point that is made by Figure 4.2 as it presents the Distribution of Economies in the geographic patterns of today.

The world map can only show highly generalized patterns of basic economies as it compares the basic forms of livelihood region by region. Figure 4.2 presents Europe and a triangular-shaped area of the Soviet Union as being within the area of "machine civilizations." All of the United States and the well-settled areas of Canada make up another extensive region which has a high form of industrial development. Less

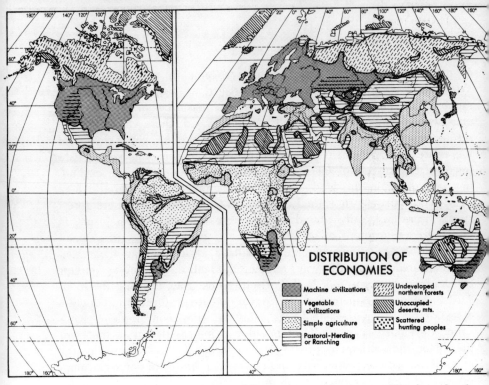

DISTRIBUTION OF
ECONOMIES

Machine civilizations   Undeveloped northern forests

Vegetable civilizations   Unoccupied deserts, mts.

Simple agriculture   Scattered hunting peoples

Pastoral-Herding or Ranching

The changing character of the world's economies makes it very difficult to classify some regions. In general, the main criterion is the extent of territory or the occupation of the largest number of people. Within any region, some people follow an economy other than the main classification, either higher or lower on the scale. Eastern Saudi Arabia, with its oil wells, might be considered an adjunct of the machine civilization. Its oases support many agricultural people, but the use of most of the land classifies it as pastoral.

FIGURE 4.2. Distribution of Economies

Source: Joseph Bixby Hoyt, *Man and the Earth*, 2nd ed., © 1967, p. 10. Reprinted by permission of Prentice-Hall, Inc., Englewood Cliffs, New Jersey.

extensive areas form the cores of settlement in Australia and New Zealand, South Africa, and the most populous communities of South America. The Orient generally is lacking in having extensive regions with a dominating "machine civilization." All of Japan is so designated, and India has two such urbanized areas for Calcutta and Bombay.

Vast regions are mapped for their dominating economies which indicate different forms of land use. Agriculture and pastoral occupance are of special significance. Also, the map shows the partly developed northern forested lands and some regions with only scattered population groups who live with a primitive hunting form of livelihood. Barriers are presented where the mountains or deserts offer a severe handicap for any kind of development. Yet it is in some of these areas that subsidized communities may obtain a commodity that enters world trade and has a high value for the industrialized areas.

It is impossible to map clearly a pattern of basic economies in more than generalizations. Within the regions shown as machine civilizations, there are the most highly industrialized communities that exist today. However, there is within these same regions almost the entire complex of other forms of livelihood. Agriculture is highly developed in its specializations and its practices; livestock raising is a highly organized operation; and mines and timbered areas are worked efficiently to provide their production for the greater settlement. Besides, there are many thousands of workers who are engaged in serving the greater community. Transportation and communication media must be a part of the complex. Trade and commerce within the regions and with other world regions are major parts of the whole. There is need for a large group of employed persons in various professions and services. The higher stages of sequent occupance require more specialized members of the economic organization than the simpler stages of the settlement.

A representation of the occupational structure of differing communities of the world offers an index of the degree of industrialization within separate world regions. TABLE 4.1 compares the percentages of employment in basic occupations for selected countries of the world. The tabulation favors the countries from within the areas of "machine civilization," Figure 4.2, and gives comparisons of the employment ratio with that of other giant countries with great total populations.

Both the United States and Canada have a strong employment in Agriculture and about one-fourth of their working population employed in Manufacturing. Europe, in its total area, has more than twice the

TABLE 4.1
OCCUPATIONAL STRUCTURE OF SELECTED AREAS°
Percent of Total Employed

Country or Region	Agriculture	Manufacturing	Handicrafts	Mining	Construction	Trade and Commerce	Trans. and Com'n	Services Others
United States	12	27	-	2	6	18	7	28
Canada	19	26	-	2	6	16	8	23
Europe Total	42	24	-	2	4	9	4	15
Great Britain	5	37	-	4	6	14	8	26
Soviet Union	55	13	4	3	3	5	4	16
India	70	2	8	-	1	6	2	11
China	75	-	5	-	-	5	1	14
Brazil	59	6	5	1	2	6	5	16

°Data tabulated from graph series on the map.

Source: Edward B. Espenshade, Jr., Editor, *Goode's World Atlas*, 12th ed. (Chicago: Copyright by Rand McNally and Company, 1964), pp. 22-23. (Used by permission of the publisher.)

proportion of its workers engaged in Agriculture as Anglo-America. However, that continent has almost the same proportion in Manufacturing as have the industrialized countries across the Atlantic. The difference in the employment ratio is made with lesser employment in the Services and the Trade and Transportation categories. Great Britain is highly specialized within its continent as a manufacturing and trading country. Ratios of employment are similar to those of the United States in all but the Agriculture and the Manufacturing totals. Great Britain has barely five percent of its workers employed in Agriculture but thirty-seven percent is engaged in some form of Manufacturing. Trade and Commerce remain high, with one British worker out of seven thus engaged.

The Soviet Union has a remarkably high total of its workers engaged in Agriculture, resembling more the occupational structure of Asia and South America than that of western Europe. More than half of the Soviet Union's labor force is employed in Agriculture and thirteen percent in Manufacturing, numbers four times as great as the proportion of agricultural workers in Anglo-America but scheduling only half as many for manufactural employment.

India and China each have about three-fourths of their labor force devoted to use of the land itself. Their employment in Manufacturing is very small indeed. It is noteworthy that workers in Handicrafts are more numerous than in the industrial program that is built more along Westernized lines. Because the numbers of their populations are so great, there is a large number of industrially employed people in both countries. The proportion in Manufacturing is low, however, and the drives to make agriculture more productive with the use of fewer workers, to release them for industrial employment, is a long-time program impossible to achieve in the near future.

Brazil's ratios of employment are between those of Asia and the pattern of industrialized nations. The ratio in Agriculture is high, while Manufacturing and Handicrafts employ a significant number of workers. Other categories of employment need larger proportions of the labor force as the country progresses into a new industrial program.

Application of westernized definitions to the patterns of sequent occupance is hardly fair as one examines the occupational patterns of other countries. A great deal of the difference is dependent upon the choices of the people concerned as to the degree to which they wish to develop their industrial program. Japan is a country in the Orient which has emphasized its industry, and it is still noted as having about one-fourth of its working population employed in Agriculture. Their living standard is high, and they are supporting one hundred million people on a land area of 143,000 square miles. Arable land makes up only one-fifth of the total area, a proportion and an acreage that match California. And yet, California has only one-fifth the population of Japan!

agricultural employment in world settlement

More than half of the working population of the world is employed in agriculture. Human settlement uses the land. The land must provide most of the foods besides fibres and industrial raw materials of many kinds. Using the land is a basic occupation and a critical form of employment. Surprisingly, its practices vary in form more than any other human endeavor. Neolithic types of farming still are practiced; some groups still use sticks and shell hoes for tools. By contrast, many American farms are almost completely mechanized, equipped with thousands of dollars worth of power equipment and machinery. In the first instance, agricultural production is for subsistence, using many workers to provide for the needs of the group. In the latter case, a very few workers can produce enough for hundreds of others who need the food and other agricultural products. Generally speaking it is the countries which are underdeveloped which have a high proportion of their population dependent upon agriculture. Highly developed countries use more of their workers for other occupations.

The measurement of agriculture's importance in the economic structure of different countries may be shown in two ways: first, the proportion of gross domestic product which is derived from agriculture and, second, the percent of the population which is engaged in agriculture. Figure 4.3 presents graphically the record of 28 countries according to these indices. The author of the graph, Thoman, makes a very significant observation, saying, "For every nation shown, labor force in agriculture exceeds gross domestic product from agriculture—that is, a higher percentage of the labor force is engaged in agriculture than that occupation yields in financial returns to the economy. Other sources must be yielding more revenue, yet hiring fewer workers."[1]

Developing countries representing each continent have long lines on the graph, Figure 4.3, signifying a high degree of dependence on agricultural employment and production. Honduras in Central America has over eighty percent of its population dependent upon agriculture, a higher share than that of any country shown. Yet its agriculture provides only half of the gross domestic product. Only a few other countries represented show as high a proportion of the economic structure based on agricultural production. Paraguay matches Honduras, while India, Turkey, and the Philippines reach almost the same figure. Pakistan is noted as having nearly sixty percent of its gross domestic product derived from agricultural effort, the highest of any of the countries

---

[1]Richard S. Thoman, *The Geography of Economic Activity*, 1st ed. (New York: McGraw-Hill Book Company, 1962), p. 277. (Used by permission of the publisher.)

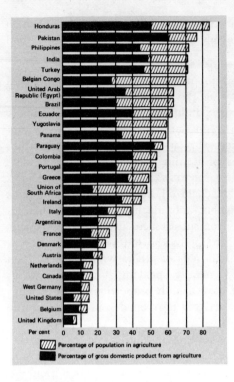

FIGURE 4.3. Percent of Population in Agriculture and Productivity, Selected Countries

Source: Richard S. Thoman. *The Geography of Economic Activity*, 1st ed. (New York: McGraw-Hill Book Company, 1962), p. 277. (Used by permission of the publisher.)

represented. India and Brazil, already shown by TABLE 4.1 as having high proportions of employment in agriculture, are giant countries whose economy is still underdeveloped in other forms of activity. Their agricultural efforts dominate the employment and production. Two other giant countries from TABLE 4.1, the Soviet Union and China, are not shown in review among the countries represented for Figure 4.3. They both have the agricultural structure playing an especially high part of their economies.

The United Kingdom is the most specialized in non-agricultural-based occupations and production of any country represented. Only about eight percent of the labor force is engaged in agriculture, with that production representing only five percent of that of the entire country. The United States and Canada, both countries with extensive farm land areas, use about fifteen percent of their workers in agriculture. The share of gross domestic production differs, however, because the larger population of the United States and the greater industrial structure there provide a high share of manufactural productivity.

Several other countries whose agricultural employment is closely related to agriculture have some significant relationships recorded by the graphs. France is more dependent upon agriculture than most of the north European countries shown. The Republic of Ireland is remarkably different from the United Kingdom. Southern Europe, represented by Italy, Portugal, and Greece, are far more agriculturally oriented than northern Europe. The Republic of South Africa presents a very different case, with high employment in agriculture (nearly fifty percent of the labor force) but with only about seventeen percent of the gross domestic product from that source. It is the productivity of the mines, employing relatively few workers, which changes the balance of production values.

The agricultural occupation is basic to the world's people. The structure of the settlement emphasizes use of the land. Its production is important to the livelihood and the personal well-being of all human population. It accompanies all other forms of activity, whether the major effort of a community is an industrial effort or one producing a mineral, a forest product, or a product from the sea. Agriculture is a stage of sequent occupance itself, but it is a form of activity which accompanies other specialized stages in the sequence. It is urgent for the student to recognize its place in relationship to the pattern of industrialization and accompanying settlement which seems at this time in the late twentieth century to be the ultimate stage in sequent occupance. A combination of the industrial stage of occupance (Secondary), other forms of activity providing Primary Services (Agricultural and Organic-extractive), along with the Tertiary (Contributory or Services) sector round out the occupational structure of the settlement.

industrial employment in world settlement

World regions which have the highest economic development are those which have well developed industrial programs. The preceding section indicates that agriculture provides a varying income for its workers, and in some countries it provides a high living standard. The same may be said of other primary or extractive industries, although they never employ so high a proportion of the labor force. The manufactural effort and the activities related to it, such as transportation-communication and trade-commerce, provide for the highest national incomes of countries and of peoples. A world map of income at national and regional levels is a record of the degree to which world communities have advanced in their form of livelihood to the final stage of sequent occupance, which is a specialization in manufactural and industrial employment.

The map of national incomes presents a far different distribution than the world population map. Figure 4.4 is a map prepared to show in three general categories the sources of national income. It is a comparison of the productivity of the world as shown by national incomes. The world is divided into nine great regions in order to make the presentation. Graphs are made for each region, with segments of each recording income from Primary, Secondary, and Tertiary sources.[2] The sizes of the pie graphs are proportioned to show for each region a comparison of the national incomes for the countries included with those of other regions. This graphic presentation compares total national incomes for world regions, and shows the share of each which come from different forms of employment.

The data plotted on the world map shown in Figure 4.4 are also shown in a graph prepared by Hoffman for a table used in his text and which is shown in this chapter as TABLE 4.2. His footnote to the table (quoted below) is especially valuable as it summarizes the criteria used for Primary, Secondary, and Tertiary sectors of the national income.

> National income equals value-added by the factors of production (*i.e.*, land, labor, capital, enterprise, and government). The primary or agricultural sector includes stock-raising, forestry, and fishing-hunting-gathering. The secondary or industrial sector includes manufacturing, handicrafts, mining, utilities, and construction activities. The tertiary or services sector includes distribution (transportation-communications and trade-commerce), non-governmental professional-personal, and governmental services.

The graphs for two great world regions dominate the map of world national income. They are those of North America and of Western Europe whose combined totals constitute sixty percent of the incomes of all the world's working peoples. Both regions have a comparatively small segment of their production from Primary sources. The Secondary sector is large for both, representing the contribution of their industrial programs; Western Europe shows more than half from this category, and North America's share is 42.5 percent. An important difference is shown by the shares of the two regions' income from Tertiary sources. Alone among all of the regions, North America has more than half of its total derived from services that are related to non-extractive and non-industrial sources. This is a response to the great size of the North American region, to the newness of the economic structure, and to the low population density of the region as it compares with that of Western Europe and several other of the world regions.

The world region of Eastern Europe and the Soviet Union has a combined national income of its countries totaling about one-half of that of North America. In that region, however, the share of the total which is derived from the industrial segment of the economy is 53.5

---

[2]Lawrence A. Hoffman, *Economic Geography*, © 1965. Pp. 12 & 14. The Ronald Press Company, New York. (Used by permission of the publisher.)

percent, the highest of that for any world region. Tertiary services are correspondingly smaller, with a lower share than for Western Europe and considerably less than for North America. Distributional services are less developed in the Soviet Union than in the United States and Canada. Primary income totals are a greater share of the economic structure than for either Western Europe or North America. This difference in the proportions of the graph segments is very like the differences shown earlier with the evaluation of the occupational structure, TABLE 4.1.

By comparison with the three largest graphs on the map, all other diagrams shown on Figure 4.4 are very small in size. Japan and India are both included within the region outlined for the "Non-Communist Far East." Japan's great industrial structure, India's vast population (although with very low per capita income), and the labor force and the productivity of Southeast Asia all combine to make the graph fourth in size among the nine great regions. Latin America is fifth, with its national income combining to more than match that of the Communist Far East. This is the record despite the fact that the population total of the South and Central American countries is less than half of that of Communist China. The Middle East and North Africa region ranks fifth in the national income totals although the region is extensive and it has a large population within its countries. Sub-Saharan Africa is one of the most extensive territories of any of the nine regions. Despite its great area, the combined national income is quite small in total ranking. Oceania, despite a high per capita income for a very small total population, has a national income that is far below the averages for the world's westernized countries. The limited numbers of people in this settlement are indicated by the national income totals.

Measurement by national income is a valid one for assessing the progress of world regions in their stages of sequent occupance. TABLE 4.2 presents quantitatively the statistics which are offered in Figure 4.4. The economic dominance of countries with high national incomes is demonstrated by the figures which review the incomes comparatively in equivalents of U. S. dollars. Different segments of the economy, deriving basic income from Primary, Secondary, or Tertiary sectors, are shown in percentages. The contrasts are apparent among industrialized regions and those which recently have begun their modernization programs. A comparison with the occupational structure of countries within these great world income regions shows how manufactural employment contributes to total income which can be measured and mapped in world-wide distributions. The world's developing countries are working hard to bring themselves into a stage of sequent occupance which will provide industrial employment and an industrialized program of their own.

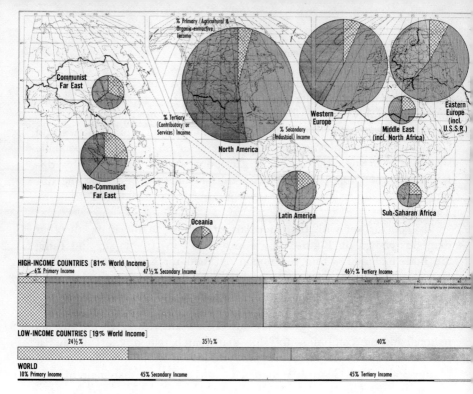

*World: National Income (Value-added), by Great-Region and
Economic-Type of Society, 1962-1964 Average-Annual (U.S. $ Billion)*

FIGURE 4.4. National Income by World Regions

Source: Lawrence A. Hoffman, *Economic Geography*, © 1965, p. 12. The Ronald Press Company,
New York. (Used by permission of the publisher.)

An accompaniment of the world's industrialization program has been
its utilization of inanimate energy. Men long ago learned that they
needed to use more energy than their physical strength could provide.
Use of animal power was the first effort. With animal domestication
and use came a long series of inventions. Domesticated animals provided draft use, mounts for riding and speedy travel for couriers or
warriors. Water and wind were used, too, as men invented water wheels,
windmills, and sails. The use of inanimate energy came late, as noted
by the study of the record of man's inventions. The use of fuels in
significant amounts for power came last of all. Fuels have been used
from Paleolithic times for warmth but not for power energy. A long
series of inventions has created an industrial program so that today
every living person has the equivalent of hundreds of human helpers
to assist him.

Developed countries with high stages of industrial development produced more energy from inanimate sources than those early in their industrial stage of occupance. The improvement of the standard of living
depends upon improved use of inanimate energy. Thus it is that new

TABLE 4.2
WORLD NATIONAL INCOME, BY GREAT REGIONS, 1962-64
World: National Income and Its Sector Composition, by Great-Region and Economic-Type of Society, 1962-1964 Average-Annual (in billions of United States dollars)

	Total Income (U.S. $ billion = 100.0 percent)	Primary (Agricultural and Organic-extractive) Sector	Secondary (Industrial) Sector	Tertiary (Contributory or Services) Sector
North America	530	5.0%	42.5%	52.5%
Western Europe	340	6.5	51.5	42.0
Eastern Europe (including the U.S.S.R.)	280	8.0	53.5	38.5
Oceania		16.5	39.0	44.5
Latin Ame		17.0	35.5	47.5
Sub-Sahar:		25.0	28.0	47.0
Middle Eas (includ:		23.5	30.0	46.5
Non-Comn		26.0	35.0	39.0
Communis		31.0	33.5	35.5
World		10.0	45.0	45.0
High-incom		6.0	47.5	46.5
Low-incom		24.5	35.5	40.0
- - - - - - - - -		(percent of U.S. $138.5 billion)	(percent of U.S.$646.0 billion)	(percent of U.S. $648.5 billion)
North Amen		19.5	34.8	42.8
Western Eur		15.9	27.1	22.0
Eastern Euro (including ue U.S.S.R.)	19.5	15.9	23.2	16.7
Oceania	1.2	2.3	1.1	1.2
Latin America	4.5	7.9	3.6	4.8
Sub-Saharan Africa	1.8	4.6	1.1	1.7
Middle East (including North Africa)	2.1	5.0	1.4	2.1
Non-Communist Far East	7.0	18.8	5.4	6.0
Communist Far East	3.2	10.1	2.3	2.5
World	100.0	100.0	100.0	100.0
High-income countries	81.0	52.0	85.0	83.0
Low-income countries	19.0	48.0	15.0	17.0

Source: Lawrence A. Hoffman, *Economic Geography*, © 1965, p. 14. The Ronald Press Company, New York. (Used by permission of the publisher.)

developments in the use of energy are studied and experimented upon in every country in the world.

Wide differences exist among the world's peoples in the amount of inanimate energy they produce and which they utilize in their own patterns of living. A useful statistical tool has been developed fairly recently by which forms of energy from other sources are converted into the equivalent of that produced by coal. The energy equivalent for tons, metric tons, kilograms, or pounds of coal can scale the energy derived from petroleum, natural gas, hydro power, or even nuclear energy. Animal power is sometimes equated into the same units. The measurement becomes valuable when comparisons are to be made among energy production figures for continents, countries, or as per capita values.

Two tables are presented to show the production and the consumption of energy within the continental regions of the world and within selected countries. TABLE 4.3 is a summary of the amount of energy produced within continent-sized world regions. The four major energy sources made up a total of more than four billion tons of coal equivalent for the date, 1960. That was about one and one-sixth tons of coal energy for each person living on earth at that time, by the production of inanimate fuels and hydro power. North America leads the world in production of energy, producing more than one-third of the world total. Caribbean America is a heavy producer also and is able to export much of its energy in its petroleum shipments. Western Europe is a leading producer especially for its coal production and a well-developed system of hydro installations. The Middle East exports great quantities of petroleum to other regions, particularly to Europe, so that the per capita production of energy column shows the quantities shipped away instead of only the quantities used by that region's own industries.

TABLE 4.3
ENERGY PRODUCED BY CONTINENTAL REGIONS, 1960
(*In millions of metric tons coal equivalent*)

Region	Total	Coal	Oil	Gas	Hydro	Per Capita Consumption*
World	4311	2204	1399	622	86	2,385
North America	1441	401	508	500	32	17,200
Caribbean America	263	5	237	20	1	1,969
Other America	34	4	23	4	3	1,144
Western Europe	563	499	20	16	28	5,655
Middle East	351	5	345	1	0	582
Far East	165	115	36	5	9	534
Oceania	31	30	0	0	1	6,497
Africa	58	43	14	0	1	683

*Per capita consumption in pounds.

Modified from: Samuel N. Dicken and Forrest R. Pitts, *Introduction to Human Geography* (Waltham, Massachusetts: Blaisdell Publishing Company, A Division of Ginn and Company, 1963), p. 84. Reprinted by permission of the publisher.

The second tabulation, TABLE 4.4, shows (for a list of selected countries) the per capita consumption of energy, again using the equivalent of coal fuel. This table ranks fifteen countries that are highest on the list of power energy consumption. The United States and Canada rank as leaders. The high energy consumption of Anglo-American countries and the relatively lower population totals as compared with those of

TABLE 4.4
PER CAPITA ENERGY CONSUMPTION, SELECTED COUNTRIES, 1964
(*Consumption in Coal Equivalent Units*)

Country	Pounds	Country	Pounds
United States	19,300	Poland	7,750
Canada	15,700	U.S.S.R.	7,550
United Kingdom	11,200	France	6,450
Belgium	10,700	Republic of	
		South Africa	5,650
Australia	9,800	Puerto Rico	3,900
West Germany	9,300	Japan	3,650
Denmark	8,700	Argentina	2,740
Norway	7,800		

Source: Joseph Bixby Hoyt, *Man and the Earth*, 2nd ed., © 1967, p. 415. Reprinted by permission of Prentice-Hall, Inc., Englewood Cliffs, New Jersey.
Data from the table from United Nations, *Statistical Yearbook*, 1965, Table 142, pp. 347ff.

Europe and Asia attest to their high degree of industrialization. Their energy consumption is about eight to ten tons per capita as used for all purposes.

Countries of Europe are other leaders in consumption of energy. Western European countries represented are United Kingdom, Belgium, West Germany, Denmark, Norway, and France. Poland and the Soviet Union are shown to have substantial totals, also. Australia is shown favorably here, for industrialization is well established in that extensive but yet not densely settled continent. Latin America has two countries represented: Puerto Rico in the Caribbean area and Argentina. Africa is represented by the Republic of South Africa. Japan is the only Asiatic country listed among the world leaders in their status as industrialized countries.

The use of energy varies from country to country, depending upon many local conditions and upon the manner of living and the industrial programs within the areas. An example is the effect of climate on energy consumption for heating and air conditioning. Estimates are as high as twenty percent of the fuel energy consumption in the United States being required for space heating. Much of the energy is used for metallurgical industries of every kind and for mass transportation media, and a great amount is used for private automobiles. Other countries utilize the energy differently, according to the forms of their industrial and manufactural program and according to the domestic fuel needs of the people. It is almost a frightening idea when the amount of energy consumed is scaled into a simple comparison. Glover and Cornell have made the following notes on the subject:

> Few persons realize the enormous energy contained in 1 pound of coal. It is four or five times that of 1 pound of T. N. T., and 1 ton of water must fall 1 mile to develop its energy equivalent. Even when it

is considered that only one-third of the energy in the coal eventually is transformed into electrical energy, it still holds true that 1 ton of water must fall 1/3 of a mile to produce in electrical form the energy that can be generated from 1 pound of coal. As a comparison, it is interesting to note that the entire flow of Niagara Falls is equivalent to an imaginary stream of coal only 18 inches in diameter.[3]

The two tables, 4.3 and 4.4, do not record the amounts of energy which are still derived from the use of draft animals nor the man-power energy which is so much a part of the activity in many developing countries. The use of human porters, of wheelbarrows, of pedicabs, of bicycles, and of hand tillage tools for agriculture, and thousands of other examples attest to the ingenuity of man as he goes about his daily life in his own locale. For the great forms of an industrial pro-gram to develop, it is impossible at this time for there to be anything less than the use of inanimate energy along Westernized lines. Nuclear energy sources in operation today are adjuncts of the industrial pro-gram which utilizes the same fuels so much depended upon by North America and Europe. The industrial form of occupance will continue to require vast quantities of energy like that used today. Developing countries must have a way of furthering their capacity to use inanimate energy as they achieve an industrial program that will increase the living standards of their peoples.

Standards of Living in World Settlement

Cultural patterns of world settlement show a great deal of the record of individual people and their living within the occupational structure of the world's regions and countries. Many evidences of people's well-being, their activities, their health, and their incomes are shown among the basic statistical summaries which relate to human settlement. Some of these items are related to the stage of cultural development of the region. Others relate to the utilization of local resources or to the man-ner in which the population deals with natural features which are im-portant in derivation of the food supply. Health and life expectancy are related to a region's basic occupations and living. Literacy and edu-cation and also personal income and nationality are other patterns which are significant in representing the standard of living of individual people within the structures of human settlement.

It is the purpose of this section of the study to review several sets of data which portray in total a comparison of living standards within the world's regions. Graphs and tables have been prepared for many publications which relate to the major topic at hand. It is necessary

---

[3]John George Glover and William Brouck Cornell, *The Development of American Industries*, 2nd ed., © 1951, pp. 613-14. Reprinted by permission of Prentice-Hall, Inc., Englewood Cliffs, New Jersey.

to examine these data within the framework of the total population distribution, dense in some regions and sparse in others, and within the occupational patterns which have already been presented in this chapter. Besides, the physical factors of the problem are involved. It is necessary to consider along with the current materials the restrictions and advantages which are offered by the major Geographic Bases of Settlement, already described in Chapter 3 of this study.

individual income

A study of per capita income is a comparative measurement of the economic status of the world's peoples. It represents the degree of participation of the population within the working and trading parts of the international economy. People within their own communities are engaged in their own occupations; they have their own share of a livelihood structure that must provide each one with his basic needs. All people participate in a system of trade, exchange, and credit. In most instances monetary transactions relate to everyone, as with payment for goods, payment for services, payment of wages, or other forms of increment. Often some form of barter is involved to provide part of the individual income. All kinds of arrangements are made to provide each person and each family with its needs of food, clothing, shelter, transportation, and the extras which relate to living.

The economies of separate countries and regions vary intensely in the income that is available to their peoples. Simple forms of agriculture, hardly above subsistence level, may provide incomes which are very low when measured on a monetary per capita basis, yet that type of economy provides a living. Still such areas may have an occupational structure developed so there is some production of surpluses that may be sold or bartered away. Surplus items eventually become a part of the world's trade goods. At the other extreme, the industrialized stage of occupance in developed countries provides the highest per capita income of all, and almost everything used in living is obtained through the use of money and credit.

Many evidences of underdevelopment and maladjustment of the economic structure of regions and of individual countries are to be observed by examining the record of per capita income. It would be impossible now or at a later date to anticipate a world-wide economic structure which would rule out those inequalities. It is to be noted that the map patterns of Figure 4.1 agree quite closely with the tabulations for per capita incomes of peoples in individual countries of the world for which such records are available.

A partial list of per capita incomes by continental areas and by selected countries is shown with TABLE 4.5. The average world income per capita was almost $500 annually, by 1965 estimates. It may be seen that there is a great difference among major world regions. North America, Australia and New Zealand, and Europe, all regions with highly developed industrialized forms of economy, far exceed the world figure. The Soviet Union ranks next with a per capita figure almost twice the world mean. The other three great world regions rank far below the leaders, some of them woefully inadequate income figures for their peoples. Some usual values are recorded within those developing regions. For an example, Kuwait is a small nation in the Middle East which has an unusually high income because of its fabulously rich oil fields. Tanzania and Nigeria, both newer nations in Africa, have far lower incomes than South Africa. India's income is far below that of industrialized Japan. Argentina and Chile are leaders in Latin America.

The measurement of per capita income is at once a mark of progress for the country and region and is a measurement of the living standards which the population must accept. It is the very nature of the economic organization that some countries must be withdrawn from world trade and communication to a high degree, while the livelihood of other countries depends upon international relationships.

food supply and dietary patterns

Providing a food supply for its population is the major effort of every area of human settlement. First, there must be enough food if

TABLE 4.5
PER CAPITA INCOME, CONTINENTS AND SELECTED COUNTRIES
(*For 1965, Most Cases*: *United States Dollars*)

Country	Income	Country	Income
World	$ 493	**Latin America**	$ 344
		Mexico	412
Africa	$ 123	Panama	425
United Arab Republic	130	Honduras	194
Nigeria	63	Argentina	740
Tanzania	64	Brazil	217
South Africa	509	Chile	515
Asia	$ 128	**Europe**	$1069
Kuwait	3184	United Kingdom	1451
Israel	1067	France	1436
Jordan	179	West Germany	1447
Iran	211	East Germany	1240
India	86	Italy	883
Japan	696	Spain	394
Northern America	$2793	**Oceania** (Aust. and N.Z.)	$1636
Canada	1825		
United States	2893	**U.S.S.R.**	$ 928

Source: Population Reference Bureau, Inc., Information Service, "World Population Data Sheet—1968," Washington, D. C., March, 1968. (Used by permission of the publisher.)

all of the people are to live well. Second, the foods themselves must be those that are acceptable to the residents of each region. The choice of food and the consumption of food are dependent upon what the area can provide to its population. For the foods which are produced locally, basic physical geography is all-important. Climatic conditions, soils and soil quality, terrain and physical land features, and even potential artificial drainage or irrigation may encourage or restrict production of many staple foods. A community may be committed to some form of regional or international trade or exchange to provide foodstuffs which cannot be produced locally, even though it may be specialized in producing a food item which is to be exported to another region. Another extremely important item in the whole relationship is the eating habits and food preferences of peoples living in individual areas.

Food supply and food preferences relate to political patterns and nationality as well as to physical and economic considerations. The economic structures of some countries can provide an adequate food supply within their areas, either from foodstuffs locally produced or from those procured abroad. Some countries can provide their own supply of foods that have a satisfactory balance of nutrients. Others may have neither the natural advantages for providing foods nor the economic status which will procure them in international trade. A low national income of the country and a low per capita income may prohibit the purchase of supplementary food supplies. A country's food resources may be limited because of an inadequate balance of nutrients and also because of the low total quantity of foodstuffs that is available to people who need it.

There has been a traditional figure often quoted regarding the quantity of food an individual requires to meet his daily needs. The estimates have been 3000 calories per day for an active working man and 2400 calories for a woman. These data were compiled for populations like those of Anglo-America and Northern Europe in latitudes where there is a need at least part of the year for extra food energy to offset the rigorous winter climates. A recent study prepared by the United Nations Food and Agricultural Organization (FAO) has revised downward those older estimates. Figure 4.5 is a set of graphs prepared after the FAO figures, showing the proportions of an "ideal diet" that is to total each day about 2400 calories per person. Also, the table shows the comparisons of that ideal diet with estimates for averages of food consumption and proportions of nutrients which are found within nineteen separate countries. As shown in the table, the balanced nutrients should provide 12.5 percent of the calories by proteins, 66.7 percent by starches and sugars, and 20.8 percent from other classes.

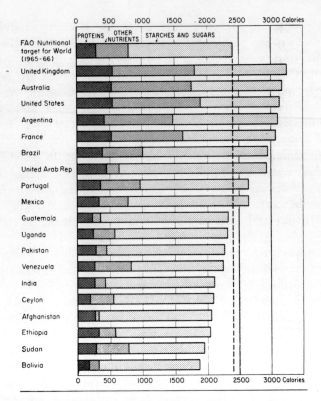

The United Nations Food and Agricultural Organization (FAO) set a world target of 2,400 calories per person in 1965-66; for a diet of reasonably good quality, 12.5 percent of these calories were to be provided by proteins, 20.8 percent by other nutrients, and 66.7 percent by sugars and starches. Few developing countries met the total caloric target in 1965-66, and fewer still consumed nutrients in the proper proportion.

FIGURE 4.5.   Quality of Diet in Selected Countries

Source: Population Reference Bureau, Inc., *Population Bulletin,* Vol. 24, No. 4 (December, 1968), p. 90. (Used by permission of the publisher.)

The countries selected for inclusion in the tables of Figure 4.5 are partly within the areas of the developed world and partly from the developing and the underdeveloped regions. Nine of the countries represented show a daily per capita food consumption greater than the proposed 2400 calories. It is to be noted that the United Kingdom, Australia, and the United States lead within this group and that for all three the amount of proteins is especially high; also, the variety of foods in the "other nutrients" classification, those which add variety to the diet, is proportionately very large. In these countries, as with France and Argentina, the dependence upon starches and sugars (which include the breadstuffs) is considerably less than that of the world averages or than the suggested norm. Brazil, Portugal, and Mexico have a high proportion of their diets made up of starches and sugars, but they have also a satisfactory amount of proteins. United Arab Republic is the unusual case. Proteins are high; however, the greater share of the diet is from the starches and sugars category. The variety of foods in between is remarkably low.

Graph sections for the ten countries whose food supply is below 2400 calories per person represent countries generally which are within the developing regions of the world, Figure 4.1. Mostly they are countries within the warm climatic regions, with some of them having very hot climates. The dependence on starches and sugars is usually quite high. Also, several of the countries have a protein supply much lower than optimum. Again, the variety of foodstuffs is cut down almost proportionally as amounts are lower than the FAO research estimates have recommended. Countries with heavy populations, especially India and Pakistan, are shown with grains and sugars very high, but with proteins considerably below dietary needs. The graphs relate in total to some significant correlations with other patterns which have been examined in this study. Figure 4.1 maps the regions with restricted development of their resource bases; the related data on national income, per capita income, and use of inanimate energy are reflected in the food supply and diets of the countries identified here for special study. It is important to note that the data graphed here are for per capita averages and totals, and not for individual persons or for families in each country. They are at best only an indication of the conditions within the countries considered. They cannot make any kind of review of the poverty written in for the millions of people who cannot have foods that are anything at all comparable to world means or which are even similar to those average data given for their own countries and regions.

The foodstuffs which form the diet of peoples in countries of the world are provided at home or are obtained by international trade. Many countries have patterns to their eating habits which are distinctive and almost "national" in their tradition. An example may be found in the use of beverages. North Europeans use traditionally great quantities of tea, coffee, and chocolate, none of which can be produced within their latitudes. Milk may or may not be a staple article of diet among the world's countries. In many countries, particularly those not highly developed, there is not enough emphasis on dairying, and there must be an acknowledgment that facilities for refrigerating and distributing fresh milk do not exist. Many countries could have the same food if they wished to do so. For example, the potato is versatile enough in its cropping adaptability to be raised much more widely than is presently the case. The cereals are important everywhere, and breadstuffs are a great proportion of the diet of almost every population group. Rice is included with the cereals in tabulation as the major grain crop of warm countries of Asia and other regions of the Old World.

A comparative record of dietary differences and eating habits within various countries is shown in TABLE 4.6. Many details are provided to support the generalizations which have been presented with Figure 4.5. As the record shows, for example, India's dependence upon cereals is very high; their meat is a very small part of the diet; and milk consumption is less than a third the per capita figures recorded for the United States or for Northern Europe. The evidence of the taboo on meat by a great part of the Indian population is indicated by the two quoted figures—milk is used but meat is not, although both foods are derived from animal sources and India has many cattle within the country.

A comparison of foodstuffs consumed in different countries and by different cultural groups shows some other interesting differences. The countries listed which use rice as the staple cereal depend on that grain more than the countries of the New World and of northern Europe depend upon their own cereal grains. Sugar is used far differently within

TABLE 4.6

CONSUMPTION OF SELECTED FOODSTUFFS FOR
SELECTED COUNTRIES, 1959-60
(*In pounds per capita per year*)*

Countries	Cereals	Potatoes	Sugar	Meat	Milk	Total Calories per day per capita
Argentina	354	154	75	240	18	3090
Australia	194	117	110	251	31	3260
Brazil	234	258	68	64	9	2640
Canada	157	139	99	181	37	3150
China (Taiwan)	344	150	20	37	-	2310
Denmark	174	282	104	161	40	3340
France	236	220	71	163	29	2940
W.Germany	183	289	64	126	29	2940
India	300	26	31	4	11	1980
Israel	271	90	64	64	20	2780
Japan	333	145	31	13	4	2210
Mexico	273	18	53	26	9	2330
New Zealand	190	121	93	236	48	3250
Peru	196	313	49	37	4	1980
UAR (Egypt)	408	18	26	29	11	2530
U. Kingdom	185	194	110	157	31	3290
United States	146	104	90	209	37	3120

*Numbers converted from kilograms used in the original table to pounds of foodstuffs per capita.

Modified from: Samuel N. Dicken and Forrest R. Pitts, *Introduction to Human Geography* (Waltham, Massachusetts: Blaisdell Publishing Company, A Division of Ginn and Company, 1963), p. 78. Reprinted by permission of the publisher.

various regions, even among peoples whose country produces its own sugar and some for export. Westernized countries consume far more than their share of sugar, obtaining much of the supply by trade. Potatoes provide an unusual record. West Germany and Denmark are high in their use of this food. So, also, are Brazil and Peru. France has a higher consumption than the United Kingdom, and both are much higher totals than for Canada, the United States, and Australia. Egypt and Mexico have the lowest consumption of this food for any countries listed, although their potential for production of this root crop is somewhat similar to several countries for which it is a staple of diet.

The eating of meat products is a highly significant part of the world's dietary pattern. Countries with considerable land available for pasture usually have high per capita consumption of meat. Notably Argentina, Australia, and New Zealand are far ahead of every other country represented in this instance. The United States and Canada still have extensive grazing lands which they can spare for raising meat animals. The United Kingdom is no longer the outstanding "beef eater" of former decades, when shipments from the world's grazing lands brought their product to British and North European markets. Meat is a high-priced food item in all but the meat-producing countries where land is extensive and where there is a relatively sparse population. Even there, other food items represent increasingly a larger share of the people's diet. In densely settled countries with a low per capita income, meat in the day's menu is too expensive for most families to procure. They usually have high proportions of the diet prepared from products of cereals and grains.

Dicken and Pitts, the same authors who have compiled the data for the table just reviewed, TABLE 4.6, have prepared an interesting graphical representation to illustrate differences in food patterns of different peoples. Figure 4.6 shows the amount of foods consumed daily by an average family in each of four countries. The countries are different in climatic conditions, in the nationality of peoples, in their cultural and occupational patterns, and in family income. In each country, also, the dietary habits are almost traditional. Regarding the data presented graphically for the countries of Denmark, Java, New Zealand, and Dominican Republic, the authors make the following summation:

> Denmark and New Zealand have a high caloric intake; Java and Dominican Republic have a somewhat lower intake. It should be noted that Denmark and New Zealand have a definite cool season, while Java and Dominican Republic have no low temperatures. (In winter the consumption of food generally is much higher.) In Denmark the average family consumes daily four pounds of cereals (mostly wheat and rye), more than four pounds of potatoes, two and one-half pounds of sugar, over one

pound of fat, five pounds of fruits and vegetables, nearly three pounds of meat, and four and one-half quarts of milk. In New Zealand the consumption of meat is much higher, that of milk is much the same, as is that of fruits and vegetables; sugar consumption is similar, but there is a lower proportion of potatoes and cereals. This intake pattern reflects the relative abundance of meat in New Zealand. In Java the daily consumption of the average family includes five pounds of rice, six pounds of sweet potatoes and bananas, a large quantity of peas and beans, relatively small amounts of fruits and vegetables, and very little sugar, fat, meat, and milk. In Dominican Republic there is a high consumption of cereals (mostly corn) and of potatoes, bananas, fruits and vegetables (peas and beans), but the consumption of meat, milk, and fats is low.[4]

The food supply of the world's peoples is a prime consideration of every governmental body and of every individual. Its improvement is the goal of every agricultural and food scientist, no matter what is his country. It is the subject most related of all to the standard of living, whether for the present or for the planned future of all parts of settlement. Provision of the food supply and a satisfactory diet for the

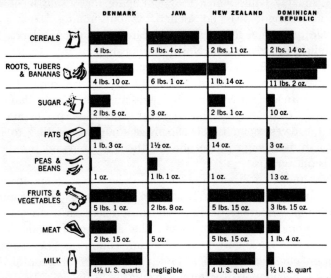

Food patterns for selected countries. The diet of a country is usually adjusted to production, but note the low recorded consumption of sugar in Java and the Dominican Republic. Additional amounts of crude sugar are probably consumed of which there is no statistical record.

FIGURE 4.6.   Food Patterns for Selected Countries

Source: Samuel N. Dicken and Forrest R. Pitts, *Introduction to Human Geography* (Waltham, Massachusetts: Blaisdell Publishing Company, A Division of Ginn and Company, 1963), p. 77. Reprinted by permission of the publisher.

---

[4]Samuel N. Dicken and Forrest R. Pitts, *Introduction to Human Geography* (Waltham, Massachusetts: Blaisdell Publishing Company, A Division of Ginn and Company, 1963), pp. 77-78. Reprinted by permission of the publisher.

population is the major effort of the century and of all time. The quality and the adequacy of people's diet relates to their health, their productivity, their attitudes, and their ability to advance themselves economically. Countries with better food and diet patterns are those who are leaders among the world's settlements.

life expectancy and health in human settlement

A study of settlement needs to present the set of distributions which shows the status of health of the population. There must be shown the conditions which result in physical and mental health and which associate with other factors to provide for the people a degree of comfortable living and opportunities to work at their chosen vocations. Health is related to many elements of daily living: to dietary patterns and food consumption; to living patterns which are adaptions to climatic conditions; to occupations and income; to disease prevalence and disease control; and finally, to medical care and services available within each community. Health measurement is difficult because it actually is almost a personal item. It is necessary to measure health almost indirectly because data specifically provided on health are inadequate. Thus a study of longevity and life expectancy trends within various countries and regions is an indication of "community health," although it is not quite a study of health itself.

Records of medical services available within different regions are other indirect measurements of the health factor. The numbers of doctors and nurses per capita for a region or district; arrangements for immunization programs, health clinics, nutritional clinics, and hospitals; and all similar statistics relate to the health of a group being considered. In the long run it is the developed countries which provide many or most of these facilities, while the newly developed regions and those still lagging far behind in these respects have unsolved health problems. It is to the credit of the governments of almost all countries and to many international agencies, supported by both public and private interests, that great forward strides in health improvement have been made during the most recent decades.

World health has improved considerably during the time period since World War II. Medical advances in the developed countries have been accelerated almost beyond belief. New medical practices and new medicines unknown a few years ago are widespread in their use. As this study is being written, there is remarkable progress in heart transplant operations. More innovations are certain to come, and the use of improved medical techniques is to become more and more extended. Medical advances and more widespread use of better medical techniques will continue to revise upward the life expectancy in every country and community. Gains in the care of infants and of their mothers at childbirth times, protection of children during early years by vaccines and antibiotics, better diets for children, and more general knowledge of basic sanitation all add to the health and well-being of the young part of the population.

Accompanying the medical advances which have preserved the lives of the very young are many new developments which have extended the lives of people in middle life and later years. Life expectancy has climbed upward as a result, with revisions of several years to be added for populations for various countries. The United Nations has presented within its series of *Demographic Yearbooks* some significant tables which show this trend during the most recent quarter century. The tables are like other measurements which attempt to represent health and physical well-being of population groups. They show life expectancy, life in years remaining beyond given ages and so, by inference, the healthiness of the people included in the statistical tabulation and analysis. In a sense, the tables present the end-product of an all-extensive cultural effort, better health for the people concerned.

Two tables from the *Demographic Yearbook* series record almost a generation of change in the life expectancy of peoples of various ages in most of the world's countries. Tabulations for eleven countries selected from the United Nations' complete lists show these data for the earliest dates available and for the latest dates. The two tables presented as TABLE 4.7 and TABLE 4.8 afford opportunity to study the changes in longevity within the differences in time. Countries selected for the tables include the United States and Canada in Anglo-America; Argentina and Mexico in Latin America; England, Wales, and Ireland (Eire) in northwestern Europe; Soviet Union; Japan and India; and two countries in Africa, Congo (Kinshasa) and United Arab Republic (Egypt). The samplings are for some of the major developed countries and for some which are now working hard to upgrade the standards of living and health for their peoples.

Data presented in the two tables show sharp contrasts between life expectancy in the developed and the underdeveloped countries. As shown throughout the UN lists, the dangers of the child's first year are very extreme. This is the case in the developed countries as well as in those whose economic structure is less well organized. In advanced countries such as in northern Europe or Anglo-America, a child surviving his first birthday may have an advantage of one to three years added to his life span. Some underdeveloped countries which lack facilities or institutions to offer assistance for infant care have a much higher mortality rate. In some of them when a child survives his first year he has five years or so added to his life. Comparison of the data for the African nations represented with those for Anglo-America illus-

TABLE 4.7
EXPECTATION OF LIFE AT SPECIFIED AGES, SELECTED COUNTRIES
Average number of years remaining to persons surviving to exact age specified.
Latest year data, before 1955.

Country Year of Data	Sex	Years of life remaining beyond age specified*									
		0	1	5	10	20	25	30	40	50	60
United States 1952	M	66.6	67.6	64.0	59.2	49.7	45.2	40.5	31.4	23.0	15.9
White Population	F	72.7	73.3	69.6	64.8	55.1	50.3	45.5	36.1	27.2	19.0
Canada	M	66.3	68.3	64.9	60.1	50.8	46.2	41.6	32.5	23.9	16.5
1950-52	F	70.8	72.3	68.8	64.0	54.1	49.7	44.9	35.6	26.8	18.6
England—Wales	M	67.3	68.4	64.7	59.9	50.2	45.5	40.8	31.4	22.5	15.0
1953	F	72.4	73.2	69.5	64.7	54.9	50.0	45.3	35.9	26.8	18.5
Ireland (Republic)	M	60.5	64.4	61.5	56.9	47.8	43.5	39.3	30.6	22.4	15.1
1945-47	F	62.4	65.5	62.5	57.9	48.8	44.7	40.5	32.1	23.9	16.4
India	M	32.5	39.0	40.9	39.0	33.0	29.8	26.6	20.5	14.9	10.1
1941-50	F	31.7	37.3	39.5	36.7	32.9	29.3	26.2	21.0	16.2	11.3
Argentina	M	56.9	61.7	59.3	54.7	45.6	41.3	36.9	28.2	20.4	13.8
1947	F	61.4	65.7	63.3	58.7	49.6	45.3	41.1	32.4	24.1	16.5
Mexico	M	37.9	44.4	48.6	53.4	37.6	34.3	31.0	24.8	19.0	13.4
1940	F	39.8	46.2	50.9	47.9	40.0	36.7	33.3	26.6	20.0	13.5
Japan	M	61.9	64.3	61.8	57.3	48.0	43.6	39.3	30.6	22.2	15.0
1953	F	65.7	67.7	65.3	60.8	51.4	47.0	42.6	33.9	25.4	17.7
Congo 1950-52	M	37.6	42.5	44.0	41.4	34.4	31.2	27.7	21.5	15.6	10.6
African Population	F	40.0	44.1	45.9	43.2	36.1	33.2	29.8	23.3	17.5	12.3
U.S.S.R.	M	41.9	51.4	54.7	51.7	43.2	39.5	35.7	28.0	21.0	14.9
1926-27	F	46.8	55.5	58.8	55.7	47.4	43.5	39.8	32.1	24.4	17.1
Egypt	M	35.7	42.1	49.8	46.9	39.8	36.4	33.0	26.1	19.4	13.3
1936-38	F	41.5	48.1	58.3	54.5	46.1	42.1	28.2	30.8	23.4	16.3

*Figures rounded to nearest tenths for data recorded in hundredths.

Source: United Nations, *Demographic Yearbook, 1955,* pp. 740-49. Copyright, United Nations (1955). (Reproduced by permission.)

trate these extreme health hazards of the very young people in each population group.

Years of life expectancy beyond the age of sixty years are not as contrasting within the UN tables as those for people within their early and middle years of life. Other tables of the demographic record would be needed to show the proportions of people within each age group. For underdeveloped countries, the age pyramids show a much lower proportion of older people than in the countries whose economic and social structures are better developed. Almost everywhere in the tables there is shown a longer life expectancy for females than for males. This is to be noticed in the data for the very young and especially for people within the upper age brackets.

The case of India's report of life expectancy presents some unusual statistical records. There has been a gain of almost ten years made during the time interval between 1941-50 and 1951-60. Health measures have improved a great deal within the time period despite a record population growth and a very heavy population load within the great country. TABLE 4.7 shows a male child at birth with a life expectancy of 32.5 years, while a girl's life might be forecast as only 31.7 years. These unusual data reoccur during the 1951-60 decade, when the years are shown respectively as 41.9 and 40.4. A great increase in years of life expectancy comes to an Indian child after he reaches his first birthday, with about seven years added. The hazards of infancy and very early childhood within the crowded population are the result of inadequate food, lack of medical care, and poor sanitation. The gains being made by the country are outstanding, however, despite the economic needs of the population that is perennially lacking in an adequate food supply.

India has another significant contrast in the life expectancy statistics in comparison with those of most other countries. As noted above, almost everywhere the expectancy of life is greater for women than men. This difference seems to be a biological fact supported by the findings of demographers and others who work closely with the subject. The records are different in India, for that country has a particularly hazardous period for its women during their years of motherhood. For example, women at the ages of 25 and 30 had in 1951-60 a life expectancy of two to three years less than their husbands. This is related to the lack of medical care' for prenatal and postnatal periods for the mothers and their children. Developed countries, even during those same age periods, show a life expectancy for women of about five years more than their mates. When the time of child-bearing is over, Indian women gain in their life expectancy so that after they have reached age 50 they become longer lived than Indian men.

Further comparisons between the two tables show more effects of the cultural structures within the different countries as they are reflected in life expectancy. Westernized cultures have far better records than those which are less economically advanced. Mexico and Argentina both are making giant strides in improving those conditions which make their populations more healthy. Japan follows the western mold, maintaining an industrialized community which can provide a reasonably high living standard and excellent public health measures. The Soviet Union has made a great deal of progress since the times of the first Five-Year Plans when there was a life expectancy matching that of today's underdeveloped countries. Data on the Congo present a need for greatly improved conditions in the living of the population. They reflect the needs of a new country that has much to do. Egypt has made very significant moves ahead in meeting basic needs for health and well-being but there, too, much more needs to be done.

literacy patterns in settlement

Ability of the world's people to communicate with each other and to read and write are the highest indices of personal, national, and

TABLE 4.8

EXPECTATION OF LIFE AT SPECIFIED AGES, SELECTED COUNTRIES

*Average number of years remaining to persons surviving to exact age specified.
Latest year data, before 1967.*

Country Year of Data	Sex	Years of Life remaining beyond age specified*									
		0	1	5	10	20	25	30	40	50	60
United States of	M	66.7	67.5	63.8	58.9	49.4	44.9	40.3	31.2	22.9	15.8
America 1966	F	73.8	74.3	70.6	65.7	56.0	51.2	46.4	37.0	28.1	20.0
Canada	M	68.4	69.5	65.8	61.0	51.5	46.9	42.2	33.0	24.3	16.7
1962-63	F	74.2	75.0	71.3	66.5	46.7	51.8	47.0	37.5	28.3	19.9
England and Wales	M	68.3	68.9	65.1	60.3	50.6	45.9	41.1	31.6	22.8	15.1
1963-65	F	74.4	74.7	71.0	66.1	56.3	51.4	46.5	37.0	27.9	19.4
Ireland (Republic)	M	68.1	69.3	65.7	60.8	51.1	46.4	41.7	32.4	23.5	15.8
1960-62	F	71.9	72.7	69.0	64.1	54.3	49.5	44.7	35.3	26.3	18.1
India	M	41.9	48.4	48.7	45.2	37.0	33.0	29.0	22.0	16.5	11.8
1951-60	F	40.4	46.0	47.0	43.8	35.6	31.6	27.9	22.4	17.5	13.0
Argentina	M	63.7	66.2	63.2	58.5	49.1	44.5	40.0	31.1	22.8	15.9
1959-61	F	68.9	71.8	68.8	64.1	54.6	50.0	45.4	36.3	28.5	19.4
Mexico	M	55.1	59.6	59.4	54.6	46.1	42.1	38.1	30.5	23.1	16.6
1956	F	57.9	62.2	62.3	58.2	49.2	45.0	40.8	32.7	24.6	17.5
Japan	M	68.4	68.8	65.2	60.4	50.8	46.1	41.5	32.3	23.6	15.7
1963	F	73.6	73.8	70.2	65.3	55.5	50.8	46.0	36.0	27.5	19.0
Congo (Kinshasa)	M	37.6	42.5	44.0	41.4	34.4	31.2	27.7	21.5	15.6	10.6
Native Pop. 1950-52	F	40.0	44.1	45.9	43.2	36.3	33.2	29.8	23.3	17.5	12.3
U.S.S.R. 1958-59	Both sexes	64.4	66.4	63.5	58.9	49.5	m45.1 f51.7	40.7	32.2	24.1	17.0
United Arab Republic	M	51.6	56.2	60.5	56.6	47.7	43.3	39.0	30.5	22.4	15.1
1960	F	53.8	59.9	66.0	62.0	52.9	48.4	43.9	35.0	26.3	18.0

*Figures rounded to nearest tenths for data recorded in hundredths.

Source: United Nations, *Demographic Yearbook*, 1962, pp. 574-83; 1963, pp. 612-25; 1964, pp. 620-23; 1967, pp. 704-41. Copyright, United Nations, 1962), (1963), (1964), (1967). (Reproduced by permission.)

international citizenship. Literacy and illiteracy measurements are important considerations in determining the status of developed, developing, and underdeveloped countries. Many elements of strength of a settlement depend upon the literacy and the amount of education of the people concerned. Occupational structure, technological programs, economic advancement, personal and national income, and even public health and physical and mental well-being all depend upon a population's being literate. The political strength of a government and of the countries within a region is dependent upon the quality of the population that comes with its being literate and thus able to participate constructively in governmental processes.

As is the case with public health, censuses present the status of the world's literacy by reverse tabulations. Tables and records usually show the proportion of the population of a country which is of persons fifteen years old or older who are unable to read and write. There are available sets of tables on illiteracy. It is this device which is used in the current study because of lack of an adequate set of data for showing the status of education as a worldwide pattern.

The Population Reference Bureau has included statistics on the world's illiteracy within its summarizing report, *World Population Data Sheet—1968*. TABLE 4.9 is excerpted from the full report, using selected countries from each continent. The list of countries shown here is the same as for TABLE 4.5, which shows per capita income. It is a remarkable fact that there is such a high correlation between the data of the two tables.

The general estimate that 39 percent of the world's population is illiterate is a critical record of the status of the cultural level of the world's peoples. The record of illiteracy varies from almost no fraction at all to a proportion of ninety percent who cannot read or write. It is within some of the countries with very high populations that the rate of illiteracy is the highest of all.

Europe has an extremely low illiteracy rate, with only five percent who cannot read and write. Northern European countries have almost no problem, but the two Mediterranean countries shown have an important percentage of their adults who lack a basic education. North American countries rank very high in their literacy quotient. Australia

TABLE 4.9
ILLITERACY RATES, CONTINENTS AND SELECTED COUNTRIES
(Population illiterate, 15 years and over, percent)

Country	Percent Illiterate	Country	Percent Illiterate
World	39%	**Latin America**	34%
		Mexico	30-35
Africa	82%	Panama	20-30
United Arab Republic	75-80	Honduras	50-60
Nigeria	80-88	Argentina	5-8
Tanzania	80-90	Brazil	30-35
South Africa	65-70	Chile	13-16
Asia	54%	**Europe**	5%
Kuwait	50-55	United Kingdom	0-1
Israel	10-15	France	0-3
Jordan	60-70	West Germany	0-1
Iran	75-85	East Germany	0-1
India	70-75	Italy	5-10
Japan	0-2	Spain	10-20
Northern America	2%	**Oceania** (Aust. and N.Z.)	0-1 %
Canada	0-3		
United States	0-3	**U.S.S.R.**	0-2 %

Source: Population Reference Bureau, Inc., Information Service, "World Population Data Sheet—1968," Washington, D. C., March, 1968. (Used by permission of the publisher.)

and New Zealand, in another region with European-type settlement, have almost no illiterate people. However, the complete table shows the other territories of Oceania with a fraction of twelve percent in the illiteracy category.

Latin America has a variable record of literacy for its population, with the division made among the countries which are classified as developing or underdeveloped countries. Argentina within Latin America has the lowest illiteracy rate of all. Its record is considerably better than that of Chile, its neighbor, and a great deal better than that of Brazil. That latter country has an estimate of illiteracy that matches that of Mexico where about one-third of the people are unable to read and write. A sharp contrast is observed for Panama when compared with Honduras, another Central American country where education is a severe problem.

Asia has more than half of its giant population listed as being illiterate. There, as in other continents, the range of difference among countries is extreme. Developed countries have a high literacy rate, with that characteristic of the population matching the economic and occupational structure of their livelihood. Japan, the most highly industrialized country in the region, has almost no illiteracy. India has barely one adult in four who can read and write. Not shown within TABLE 4.9 are the data for China. The *World Population Data Sheet—1968* shows for Mainland China 728 million persons with an illiteracy rate of 40-50 percent. Taiwan has a population total of 13.5 million, and 34-45 percent who cannot read and write.

The literacy quotient of the Soviet Union matches that of western Europe, Australia and New Zealand, and Northern America. The intensive drive which has been given to education during recent decades has resulted in an intensely low figure of illiteracy for the country and its 239 million persons.

Illiteracy rates for Africa are the highest of those for any continent. In total consideration only about one in five persons is literate according to the general estimate. This pattern is an accompaniment of the conditions which are generalized with maps such as Figure 4.2. There is a great handicap for the countries of that region as they aspire to economic growth, technological improvement, and political stability. Advances in education must be made to assure better living standards and prosperity for the peoples of that continent.

Cultural Geography of Settlement

Cultural aspects of human settlement vary from region to region over the world, registering every facet of life of man within his habitat.

Settlement varies in its form from region to region, responsive to the cultural features of the occupance structure. Cultural items are reflected in the visible forms of the settlement pattern. Settlement takes advantage of the environmental conditions which provide advantages or disadvantages within the physical setting. The element of human choice transcends. The choices depend in large part upon the background of the population groups themselves. There are highly developed cultural groups in natural settings where life is a struggle if people are to have a high standard of living. Conversely, even during this late twentieth-century period, there are many underdeveloped regions which have great potential. They have a potential resource base so that the living of all their residents could be improved far beyond present levels.

The background of the population groups has tended to restrict or to encourage improvement of the cultural structure of human settlement. The review of three basic patterns in this chapter (racial stocks, language groups, and world religions) has emphasized the element of cultural backgrounds. These three patterns have been important as they have been related to the occupational structure of the settlement. They have been important also within the observed stages of occupance within the separate world regions.

The standard of living of the world's peoples has been predicated upon the degree of acceptance of contemporary occupational patterns. For people in a densely populated area to live well they must have a form of occupance that uses the land resources to the full and which has an industrial structure also to provide employment and incomes for its residents. Developed nations and regions today are users of vast amounts of inanimate energy. Their economy yields great stores of manufactured goods which are used in the daily lives of their own people as well as providing the basis for an exchange of goods through a well organized distributional system. Industrialized communities process even the food supplies for their own consumption.

Well-being of the population of any portion of the world settlement depends upon the standard of living which the economic structure can provide. Highly developed settlements depend upon the personal advantages which the people can share. Personal incomes, items of health, literacy, and ability to participate in the economic structure and the governmental organization of nation or community, all these, and more, translate cultural values into the structure of human settlement.

Chapter 5

The Structure of
Human Settlement

Dispersal of human population is identified by the visible features of settlement. These distributions are the evidences of the livelihood structure of each separate community. They are the tangible elements on the cultural landscape. Everywhere men must have abodes for themselves, and they must have organized institutional structures by which they earn their living. Those structures may be fields or tilled areas; they may be industrial plants or warehouses. Men need buildings for social purposes and for governmental functions, for banks and for publishing houses and for housing stations which serve communication media. There is a spatial organization to the features of the settlement, all woven together by the pattern of transport and communication which is the integrating network of it all. Patterns of settlement differ from place to place and within the world landscape; there is a separate identity for each region or area. Visible differences appear between the developed and the developing regions, sometimes by degree and intensity and sometimes by the dominance of features which present clearly the specialization of the communities. The discernible features of settlement are an infinitely varied pattern in their world distributions.

Earlier chapters of this study have shown that there are today more than three billion people living on the earth. Also, the distribution of population is very uneven in its density and arrangements within world regions. Dispersed patterns of settlement, with people distributed on the land itself, form the rural component while great nodes or concentrations contain the urban population. At this period in the twentieth century, one-third of the population is contained in urban communities. Two billion people are widely dispersed in areal or regional patterns in some form of rural settlement.

As population has grown during the most recent decades, it is the trend that cities have become more and more important with each generation. Cities are of every size, from those barely meeting the lower limits of census definition to great metropolitan centers which contain as many people as the entire population of a medium-sized nation. Although they obviously are restricted in their areal extent, urban communities dominate the structure of the world settlement in a physical sense as well as in an economic relationship. There is a constantly increasing number of people who must live somewhere and who must earn incomes by working at some trade or profession or by affording other forms of service within the roster of working peoples. Again, as shown in Chapter 4, the contribution of urbanized communities is usually secondary and tertiary in nature. Cities provide the coordinating elements for the regions around them, and they serve as centers of their own areas able to intercommunicate with other nearby or distant urban communities.

The rural component of the settlement is distributed on the land, for the most part giving precedence to the arable lands of the earth. There is a high value for land which can be tilled so it can provide its production to population support. There is a special priority for lands which can be made to produce some commodity of commercial interest. Increasingly, the role of primary production for rural settlement shifts more to that of secondary and tertiary specialization. This trend is noted more and more in the highly developed countries and more by the pattern of occupations than by production of commodities for exchange. In Anglo America and in western Europe, especially, the rural elements of the settlement participate in nearly the same occupational structure as the residents of urbanized centers. In developed countries, fewer workers than ever before are able to make the land produce more of the world's trade goods than can be produced by a less well organized occupational system.

Transportation and communication systems of the world have grown along with the increase in population and with the development of an urban-dominant settlement. Transportational networks are uneven in their distribution and in their quality among world regions. As areas of settlement become more concentrated in population density and as occupational structures become better integrated within the urban areas and between the rural settlement and adjacent cities, a transportation system must keep abreast. Transportation media are coordinated so that land, air, and water carry passengers, while goods and commodities also are carried by a variety of methods. These include road and highway vehicles, planes, barges and ships, and even pipelines. Communication media help unify the functional organization of the settlement. They are coordinating agencies which distribute news, transact business and diplomatic exchanges, and supply entertainment.

The premise that man is in residence and at work in area is supported by the visible features of settlement. There are distributions which relate to the occupance of man, rural and urban elements and the transportation and communication media which serve and unite them. Smaller features are distinctive in the settlement pattern, also. These are industrial plants, dock-side facilities, airports, public buildings, office buildings, places of worship and entertainment, warehouses, shops, and stores. Roads and highways, trails and paths, air landing strips and runways, harbors, pipeline termini, railroads and staging yards, and others are all parts of the transportation network. Power lines, telephone lines and cables, transmission towers, broadcasting and relay stations are part of the communication nerve system which helps coordinate the livelihood of the settled area.

Pattern of Rural Settlement

Rural population occupies by far the greater share of the world's settled areas. It is a dispersed pattern with its livelihood usually associated with some form of extensive land use. Almost traditionally, the rural settlement has been considered the agricultural part of the occupance. However, several other forms of settlement are dispersed over extensive areas, with the numbers of people being relatively few. Examples of such settlements are communities where there is lumbering, mining, forest gathering, and even fishing. Nomadic peoples with their herds occupy other areas, usually restrictive in nature, which are able to support only a low population density. People arrange themselves within a given region often according to the resource base available. Also, they reflect their stage of economic development. Their pattern of occupance may be an early stage in their settlement or it may have matured after a long-time residence of the group within the area.

A map of population, such as the *Frontispiece* of this study, is almost a map of rural settlement. The urban population is gathered into areas of restricted size, with dense population surrounding them but giving way to lesser population density with distance from the urban foci. In the dispersed settlement, there are small nuclei of every size from hamlets to city-like communities that barely miss urban classification because of some arbitrarily-set census definition. Rural settlement is closer to the land than the urban elements of the population pattern in its activities as well as in its distribution.

Rural settlement may be distributed on the land itself in a simple pattern of migrating peoples, occupying the land only for a time before moving on or as a dispersed form where boundaries and land holdings are well identified with separate tracts for each family. Nomadic peoples are on every continent, but they number only five million or so in total number. They have been relegated to the less valuable lands for the most part, lands that are dry, dry and hot, hot and very wet, or very cold. Even nomads retain contact with major settled areas, for there is everywhere an active form of exchange and local commerce that is traditionally a part of the regional economic structure. Nomadic peoples are in contact with neighbors who remain in permanently established communities.

Rural settlement depends upon the urban part of the occupance even as it provides those same centers of population with its supplies of raw materials. The cities provide leadership, financial support, markets, and supplies of goods from afar which the rural communities could not obtain by themselves. The processing of raw materials from rural areas is done within metropolitan communities. Increasingly, in much of the world, the rural residents depend upon the urban sectors to provide employment. The occupational structure and functions of rural and urban settlement draw closer together with time, especially in the developed countries.

The rural pattern of settlement in Anglo-America includes individual farmsteads distributed upon the land itself and a set of hamlets and villages which have served their local areas. These individual land holdings, large and small, and their local trading centers have made up the pattern of American agricultural regions. The farms were formerly nearer self-sustaining than now, with houses for the farm family and other buildings which served special functions associated with farm activities. There are dairy farms, those specialized in the production of livestock, cash grain farms, and those which produce special crops (such as cotton, tobacco, or sugar beets). There are also many combinations of these and other specializations. It is important to note that the evolution of this great complex has taken place as a road system has been built to aid communication with the urban centers.

Villages and hamlets which have been a part of Anglo-America's dispersed rural settlement have interesting historic beginnings, for they usually were begun during a time in which the range of travel was much more limited than at present. They maintained themselves because of centrality of location, strategic position at a break in transportation, as at a stream crossing, at the intersection of traveled routeways, or as a center which contributed some special form of service. Examples are: villages built at a ferry, at a grist mill site, at a railroad crossing, or near a creamery, a sawmill, a blacksmith shop, or an implement dealership. Other small centers of settlement had nonfarm beginnings. Mining towns, sawmill towns, fishing villages along a lake shore or a coastal inlet, clustered housing near a power plant or at a power dam, or at a smelter—all these form a partial list of minor nodes of settlement in the rural regions of the continent.

In other continents, there are many regions which have a different pattern of rural settlement. In western Europe, especially, the nuclear farm village is a part of the settlement on the best agricultural land as well as within isolated valleys. A source of water, such as a spring or a common well, may have been the critical element in the location of the village. Also, a transportational feature, as a route in a valley, a river ford or crossing, or the entrance to a pass, may have afforded the beginning. Centers of population have survived from feudal times with a community organized around a village with its church and market place. In many instances the motive for the arrangement has been to provide for defense. Also, there has not been the high degree of freedom to move about that has come to the American farm family, so the small communities had to assume a higher degree of self-suffi-ciency than in the westernized areas.

The patterns of rural settlement have changed with the general shifts in the occupational patterns of both developed and developing regions. There is increasing contact of rural areas with urban com-munities and with larger communities that formerly were almost out of reach of the dispersed settlements which were on the land itself. In the United States, the hamlets and villages are no longer self-con-tained service units for their neighborhoods, to serve the farm com-munities, miners' families, or the cluster of homes at a railway "division station." Many are residential communities housing commuters who earn their incomes in industrialized employment or in providing some form of service which is a part of the urbanized occupational structure of the region. "Bedroom communities" are taking the place of the com-munities of the past, with their residents a part of the metropolitan and urban labor force. Farm villages of the past may be completely converted from their former activities and functions that served their rural neighborhoods.

Rural settlement shares with the total of human population in its relationship with the physical features of the landscape. The same features which make many regions inhospitable for use by a dense settlement (those described in Chapter 3) seem to work overtime in restricting the rural components of the occupance. Climatic restrictions are especially severe because the greater part of the rural settlement must use the land for its productivity. Physical restrictions keep large numbers of residents away from rugged mountain areas, from tropical rain forests, and from deserts. Dense settlement depends upon arable land. It is in communities located on the best lands available that rural settlement is concentrated. There must be proximity to urbanized or metropolitan segments of the settlement. In their own instances, they too must have the support of an arable land supply in their hinterlands. The role of rural settlement is changing rapidly in North America and Europe, and in other world regions as well, as the occupational structures of urban and rural areas draw closer together.

Features of Urban Settlement

The urban part of the settlement is the most highly organized regional structure of human occupance. Although the urban centers house only one-third of the world's peoples, they dominate the activities of the entire settlement. The proportion of the population counted as urban varies considerably from region to region and among countries of the same region. Both the developed and the developing regions differ in the share of the population which is included as urban.

Functionally, cities are different from each other as regions themselves are different. Generally, cities are busy with the secondary and tertiary services for their regions and their people. However, in many instances today there are communities of urban size and description located at the sites of vast primary production areas.

Cities are organized more closely than their rural neighborhoods. They must provide the unity of organization for the production and efforts of their hinterlands and make contacts and outlets for them. They must have an internal structure which serves the people within the cities themselves. Cities most often specialize with a particular set of functions or a combination of them. They may be secondary (as the manufacturing of clothing or automobiles) or tertiary (as a center of banking and insurance). Always there is a variety of activity, with functions of primary, secondary, and tertiary occupational effort present in the urbanized community. A great many of the city's workers must be engaged in supplying services. They are engaged in merchandising, trade, and the professions. They provide the organization of the financial, commercial, legal, and the regulatory functions needed for people to live and work together in large concentrations.

Cities are regional centers, and they also are in large measure regions within themselves. Part of their functions are internal, others are intraregional, and still others are international. Cities have identification as functional capitals. Some are trade centers, manufacturing centers, political capitals, and even religious and educational capitals. In most instances, they lead their surrounding areas in their specialized activities. They provide the organization needed to help their communities relate to others in the total pattern of rural and urban settlement.

distribution of urban population

Growth of many great cities during the twentieth century has been the most significant phenomenon of evolving settlement during recent time. The increase in population from two to three billion persons in recent decades, TABLE 2.4, has found much of the growth within the urban communities themselves and within their satellites which have joined closely with the functional structure of the larger population centers. Urban growth has accompanied the changing economic structure of the entire world settlement. It reflects the ever-increasing efficiency of the world's transportation and communications network and the sharing of exchanges of every kind among world regions.

The study of urban settlement is made difficult by the variety of definitions which have been used by different countries to classify city size. Within the United States, a community which has a population of 2,500 or more is classed as a city. Canada uses a figure of 1,000, but some countries use figures as high as 20,000 as a lower limit for urban size. In other countries, the capital may be called "urban" despite its true population number. Coming into use now are higher figures than those used for older records so that listings are prepared for urban communities of more than 20,000; 100,000 or more; a half million and above; and the giant cities of more than a million inhabitants. Another interesting plan is used by the United Nations, which has prepared tables that name cities which individual countries themselves consider "urban" sized.

Despite the problems of defining the lower limit of population required to have a community classified as "urban," there are some excellent studies today of the world's cities. TABLE 5.1 is prepared after the study of Hoffman who has worked out the proportions of urban population in the major world regions.[1] The regional delimitations used are the same as those mapped in Figure 4.4 of this study.

Hoffman's tabulations show two categories for urban population, along with the 1962-64 population totals for his "Great Regions." The columns for "Officially" Urban are obtained from United Nations sources, accepting the variety of definitions in current use. As shown, 33.2 percent of the world's people are within this category. The second set of urban data depends upon the population size of 20,000 to qualify for urban classification. By that measurement, slightly less than one-fourth of the population is urban. In both sets of data the great disparity in the proportion of urban peoples within the separate great regions is the most significant part of the table.

---

[1]Lawrence A. Hoffman, *Economic Geography*, © 1965, pp. 12 & 71. The Ronald Press Company, New York. (Used by permission of the publisher.)

TABLE 5.1

Regional and Urban Population by Great Regions and World, 1962-64

	Total Regional Population		"Officially" Urban		Population in Cities 20,000 and Over	
	Mil lions	% of World Total	Mil lions	% of Reg'al Total	Mil lions	% of Reg'al Total
Anglo America	210	6.6	150	71.5	100	47.6
Western Europe	315	9.9	190	60.3	140	44.5
Eastern Europe (incl. the U.S.S.R.)	350	11.0	171	48.8	115	32.9
Oceania	17	0.5	12	70.8	11	64.8
Latin America	220	6.9	100	45.6	55	25.0
Sub-Saharan Africa	210	6.6	25	11.9	19	9.0
Middle East (incl. North Africa)	143	4.5	40	28.0	28	19.6
Non-Communist Far East	950	29.9	240	25.3	175	18.5
Communist Far East	765	24.1	130	17.0	92	12.0
World Total	3,180	100.0	1,058	33.2	735	23.1

The world regions as delimited in this table are mapped in Figure 4.4 of this study; also, statistics for TABLE 4.2 are presented for the same regional divisions, as prepared by Hoffman.

The population figures used here are those compiled by Hoffman, and the percentages for the total regional populations are also from his tables. The percentage for the urban components of the population are separately computed.

Source: Lawrence A. Hoffman, *Economic Geography*, © 1965, pp. 12 and 71. The Ronald Press Company, New York. (Used by permission of the publisher.)

When densely populated regions are considered, the world regions facing the North Atlantic are those with the highest proportions of urban people. Oceania, principally Australia and New Zealand, with only 17 million people in all, has the highest proportion of any region living in its cities. Africa has a low share of its population urbanized, despite its large population. The most striking data of all, however, are for the Non-Communist Far East and the Communist Far East. Despite their combined population of 1.7 billion people, half of the world's total, less than one-fifth of the population lives in urban communities.

growth of urban population

Urban population increased from a proportion of about ten percent of the world's people in the mid-1920's to more than 25 percent during the present decade. The growth was made by the increase in the size of other urban areas so that they are now listed in the new tabulations for large metropolitan centers. Satellite cities are a new development, with their numbers often added to the enlarged communities so that the urban pattern is comprising more of the regions' peoples and of their area, too. Coalescing urban areas have created today's "megalopolises" in westernized countries and in the Orient also.

The number of cities which have 100,000 or more people has increased in every continental region. A study made in 1931 shows that there were 537 cities of that size category in 1927.[2] The combined population of all those world cities was 182,000,000. That number was but 9.6 percent of the world population. As TABLE 2.5 shows, the world population totaled less than two billion people for that time period. Yet only one person of ten was a resident of a large city during the decade which Jefferson reviewed.

A combination of Jefferson's data and those of Trewartha, et al., for a recent date is presented in TABLE 5.2. By 1960, there were 1,367 cities each with a population of 100,000 or more.[3] The number of large cities more than doubled, and it is certain that the population living in such large urban communities at least tripled during the time interval.

The growth of many cities with populations of more than a million people has been a phenomenon of the three most recent decades. In 1930, there were about thirty cities in the world in that classification, with nine or ten of them in Europe west of Russia. By 1960, there were nineteen European cities in the million and larger category and six more in the Soviet Union. The United States had six such cities in 1930, with a combined population of 17.6 million. By 1960, there were sixteen urbanized areas each with a million or more people. They had a combined population total of more than 50 million. New York grew from eight million to fourteen million within its urbanized area during the time interval. The next five cities in size grew as follows: Chicago, 3.4 to 5.9 millions; Philadelphia, 2.1 to 3.6 millions; Detroit, 2.0 to 3.5 millions; Los Angeles, 1.2 to 6.4 millions, changing rank to second place in size of its urbanized area's population; and Boston, 1.0 to 2.4 millions. San Francisco increased in size to join the other giants, from 624,000 in 1930, to 2.4 million in 1960, to match Boston.

Cities in tropical latitudes have likewise had extremely high rates of population growth during recent decades.[4] Their population changes are shown by a table prepared by Hoyt which lists 20 cities in the tropical regions of three continents, none of them with populations of

---

[2]Mark Jefferson, "Distribution of the World's City Folks," *Geographical Review*, Vol. 21, No. 3 (July, 1931), pp. 446-65. (Used by permission of the publisher.)

[3]Glen T. Trewartha, *et al.*, *Elements of Geography*, 5th ed. (New York: McGraw-Hill Book Company, 1967), p. 573. (Used by permission of the publisher.)

[4]Joseph Bixby Hoyt, *Man and the Earth*, 2nd ed., © 1967, p. 274. Reprinted by permission of Prentice-Hall, Inc., Englewood Cliffs, New Jersey.

TABLE 5.2

Cities with Population of More Than 100,000 by Continent

Continent	Number of Cities 1927	Number of Cities about 1960
Europe	182	524*
Asia	224†	454‡
North America	90	227
South America	20	88
Oceania	9	12
Africa	12	62
Total for World	537	1,367

*Including all USSR   ‡Excluding all USSR
†Includes all of Turkey and
  all of Russia

Sources: Mark Jefferson, "Distribution of the World's City Folks," *Geographical Review*, Vol. 21,
No. 3 (July, 1931), pp. 446-65. (Used by permission of the publisher.)
Glen T. Trewartha, *et al.*, *Element of Geography*, 5th ed. (New York: McGraw-Hill Book
Company, 1967), p. 277. (Used by permission of the publisher.)

a million in 1900, but with nine of that size in the 1960's. Figures quoted in this paragraph are from his tabulations. For example, Singapore had a 1960-64 size of nearly two million. In 1900 the population was only 228,000. Bombay grew from its 1900 population of 776,000 to a 1960-64 total of 4.4 million. Rio de Janeiro grew from 811,000 in 1900 to 3.3 million during the early 1960's. Other tropical cities in Central and South America, Africa, and Asia have made so much growth recently that they rank now among the world's greatest cities.

Japan is so highly urbanized that it has 123 cities larger than 100,000, of which three are classified within the 500,000 to one million category and six more are greater in size than a million inhabitants each.[5] Tokyo is now counted as the world's largest city, with a population of more than fifteen million persons. China, also, has many great cities, with fourteen of them larger than one million and eighteen more within the size of a half million to a million people.

The most recent world censuses show that many cities have grown to giant size during recent decades. The United Nations has recorded those urban populations in its series of *Demographic Yearbooks*. TABLE 5.3 lists great world cities from every continent. As was noted before, the actual size of the cities is at variance because of the different criteria for city boundaries. That element adds interest to the table, however, because it shows how very important the cities have become in every world region. Even those areas with less dense populations have great cities. The Middle East and Africa are examples of great urban growth within the most recent years.

---

[5]Trewartha, *op. cit.*, p. 573. Other data in this paragraph are from the same tables.

TABLE 5.3
POPULATIONS OF GREAT CITIES WITHIN EACH CONTINENT
Selected List from United Nations Tables

City	(Date of Densus)	City Population City Proper	Urban Agglomeration
Melbourne	(1966)	75,709	2,108,499
Sydney	(1966)	158,801	2,444,735
Cairo	(1966)	4,219,853	
Alexandria	(1966)	1,801,056	
Johnnesburg	(1960)	595,083	1,152,525
Germiston	(1960)	148,102	214,393
Tokyo	(1966)	8,907,000	11,005,000
Yokohama	(1966)	1,860,000	
Osaka	(1966)	3,133,000	
Seoul	(1966)	3,794,959	
Bombay	(1967)	4,902,651	
Calcutta	(1967)	3,072,196	4,764,979
Delhi	(1967)	2,511,482	2,874,454
Shanghai	(1957)	6,900,000	
Peking	(1957)	4,010,000	
Tientsin	(1957)	3,220,000	
Bangkok	(1963)		1,608,305
Djakarta	(1961)	2,906,533	
Hong Kong	(1961)	Total Population	3,133,131
		Urban Population	
		(Inc. Victoria)	2,292,621
Singapore	(1967)	1,955,600	
Teheran	(1966)	2,695,283	
Karachi	(1967)		2,721,200
Baghdad	(1965)	1,745,328	
Istanbul	(1965)	1,750,642	2,052,368
London	(1966)		7,913,600
Paris	(1962)	2,790,091	7,369,387
East Berlin	(1965)	1,073,647	
West Berlin	(1966)	2,190,577	
Budapest	(1966)	1,960,000	
Madrid	(1965)	2,599,330	
Roma	(1965)	2,484,737	
Athinai	(1961)	627,564	1,852,709
Hamburg	(1966)	1,851,327	
Moskva	(1967)	6,422,000	6,507,000
Leningrad	(1967)	3,296,000	3,706,000
Sao Paulo	(1967)	5,383,000	
Buenos Aires	(1960)	2,966,816	7,000,000
Montevideo	(1963)	1,158,632	
Bogota	(1967)	2,066,131	
Caracas	(1966)		1,764,274
Mexico City	(1967)	3,353,033	
Montreal	(1966)	1,222,255	2,436,817
Toronto	(1966)	664,584	2,158,496
Chicago	(1966)		6,732,000
New York	(1966)	7,969,000	11,410,000

Source: United Nations, *Demographic Yearbook, 1967*, pp. 172 and 207-17. Copyright, United Nations (1967). (Reproduced by permission.)

The urbanized part of the settlement has been mapped by a geographer as he outlined the world's "Urban Regions." That map, by Alexander, is included here as Figure 5.1. His map encloses with a line all the area within 100 miles of a city having a population of 100,000 or more and shades the areas where their territories coalesce. He has used two areal categories, with heavy shading for "Major Regions," and a less dense pattern for "Minor Regions." Furthermore, his map highlights the locations of cities he has designated as "super" or "millionaire" cities (those with populations of more than one million). These numbered 82 according to the 1960 census. The regional hinterlands of more than 1000 great cities and the "millionaire" cities show four great urban regions in the world and many other nodes of urban settlement. Of them, Alexander has written the following description:

1. The foremost area covers almost all of western Europe to the Mediterranean shores, and even includes the Mediterranean fringe of Morocco, Algeria, and Tunis. Eastward prongs extend beyond the Urals and over the Caucasus as far as the Persian Gulf. A southern extension penetrates Turkey and reaches Israel. Within this vast zone are no less than 38 cities of a million or more people. Great Britain alone has seven, Germany has eight, Italy four, Russia three, and the Iberian Peninsula three. In 1935 Europe had 23 of the world's 56 millionaire cities; today it contains 38 of the world's 99.

2. In eastern Asia the zone of urbanism extending from Manchuria to Indonesia contains 22 millionaire settlements. The striking thing about this region is the number of *new* supercities; 13 of them have crossed the million mark since 1935. Five of these are in mainland China, which now claims at least ten cities in the million-plus category. The tropical portion of this realm is particularly noteworthy in that every one of its supercities assumed millionaire status within the past 25 years.

3. India and Pakistan likewise are experiencing rapid growth in both the population of large cities and the number of supercities. A quarter of a century ago only Bombay and Calcutta were in the one-million-or-more category. Today Madras, Delhi, Hyderabad, Bangalore, Ahmedabad, Karachi, and Lahore have joined the ranks.

4. North America has a cluster of large cities in its eastern portion, from the St. Lawrence Valley on the north to Cuba on the south. There are several detached areas on the West Coast, in Central Mexico, and along the Pacific side of Central America. All told there are 20 millionaire cities in this part of the world.

Elsewhere, urbanism appears in nodes or short belts. The pattern in South America is peripheral, resembling a giant horseshoe with one point in Venezuela and the other in eastern Brazil. Of this continent's six millionaire settlements, three (Lima, Santiago, and Caracas) qualified just recently. Africa has no extensive urban belt except on her western Mediterranean coast; her three super settlements (Alexandria, Cairo, and Johannesburg) are at her antipodes. Spotted around in numerous parts of the continent are a few places that have passed the 100,000 mark. The two metropolises of Australia front on her eastern and southern coasts.[6]

---

[6]John W. Alexander, *Economic Geography*, © 1963, p. 520-21. Reprinted by permission of Prentice-Hall, Inc., Englewood Cliffs, New Jersey.

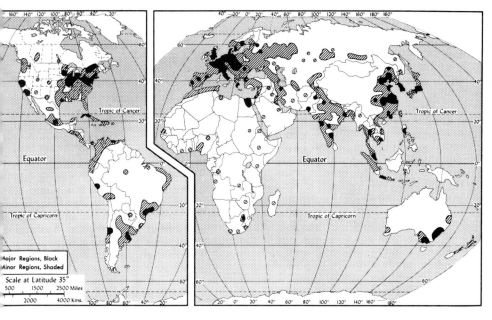

FIGURE 5.1. Urban Regions

Source: John W. Alexander, *Economic Geography,* © 1963, p. 520. Reprinted by permission of Prentice-Hall, Inc., Englewood Cliffs, New Jersey.

An accompaniment of the intensive trend toward urbanization has been the growth of today's *megalopolis*. The term has been created to describe areas where great cities and their satellite communities grow into each other, so there is a continuing extensive area of urban settlement with no rural space between. Such an area is in North America, with a great urbanized region extending from New England to the Washington, D. C., area. This region is almost joined by another area along the southern side of Lake Erie, from western Pennsylvania to Chicago and Milwaukee, south and west of the southern end of Lake Michigan, including portions of Ohio, the southern third of Michigan, and northern Indiana.

Other continents and regions have megalopolises also. Great Britain and northwestern Europe, Japan, and even India and Java have urban settlements which grow together in area and in function. The further growth of Oriental cities and megalopolises is certain to be a trend in their settlement. Japan has already reached a high degree of urbanization. The vast populations of China and India, and the concentrated settlements in favored portions of southeast Asia are doubtlessly soon to have great megalopolises like Japan.

Transportation Systems in Settlement

The transportational system is the unifying element of settlement. Foods and living necessities of all kinds must be distributed among the people of a region. People themselves must have means to get from their abodes to their places of occupation. Individual settlements are served by transportation systems within their own areas. Also, the contacts by peoples interregionally are dependent upon adequate transportation systems. People today live in three dimensions for transportation: land, water, and air. In all of these, many media of transport exist, and modern technology is creating more as well as improving upon forms of transport which have been traditional through centuries of development.

Transportation systems are developed and improved as a part of an industrialization program. Raw materials must be transported to the plants, and manufactures must be carried away to markets. Sometimes the production of an individual plant is dependent upon part of the transportation system which is far-reaching or world-wide. Supplies of commodities are moved from region to region and from country to country. They must be freely distributed within their own area, too, serving the local as well as the larger settlement.

A basic difference between developed, developing, and underdeveloped regions is found in the form and the adequacy of the transportational network. All forms of transportation are important. The contrasts between footpaths and superhighways, camel trails and airstrips, sampans and steamships are related to the economic development of world regions.

basic patterns of transportation

Every area of settlement has its transportational network, serving its own area and linking it to other communities near and far so there can be a functional organization to the occupance structure. There are sets of lines for the routeways themselves, weaving the community together and integrating different media into a total network. There are terminals for every medium: railway stations and railyards, ocean harbors, airports, and pipeline stations. The different forms of transport supplement each other functionally, within an individual region as well as within the total pattern of settlement.

Roads and Highways

Some form of roads serve every portion of human settlement. There are footpaths that converge into trails and trails which lead to roads in every region where people live. There are many more of the tiny trails than can be mapped which accompany a simple form of settlement. Yet, it is those paths which are an intrinsic part of the basic rural settlement of many countries, particularly those which are underde-

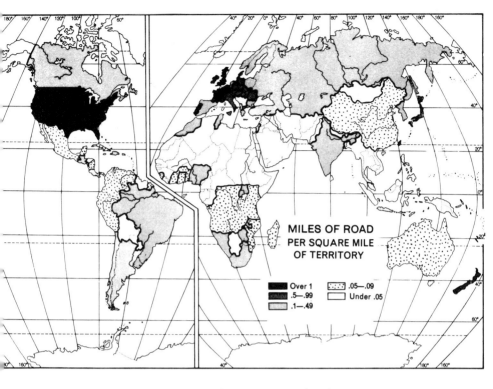

FIGURE 5.2. Miles of Road Per Square Mile of Territory

Source: Joseph Bixby Hoyt, *Man and the Earth*, 2nd ed., © 1967, p. 26. Reprinted by permission of Prentice-Hall, Inc., Englewood Cliffs, New Jersey.

veloped. Perhaps if the quality of roads is ignored, the density of the road network in most areas of settlement would be nearly the same. It would certainly be an appropriate combination to match with a detailed pattern of population distribution, for the paths between man's abode and his places of work and sources of his necessities are elements in his daily living.

The system of improved roads is a pattern which geographers have been able to map and to study in some detail for the world's regions. Except on very large scale maps, the road pattern must be generalized in order to have meaning as a mappable feature. The map presented as Figure 5.2 shows miles of road per square mile of territory by national areas. This has a shortcoming in that no intra-national locations are shown, where roads are adequate and where they are not. It can only partially show the true pattern in countries that have population concentrations in restricted portions and which may have those areas very well served or, perhaps, have a very poor beginning of a network of improved roads.

Two regions are especially well served by improved roads; they are northwestern Europe and the United States. Both regions have more than one mile of surfaced road per square mile of territory. That means that the area of one section has a road to share with nearby land, thereby providing a splendid network. That the adjacent area of Canada, attached to northwestern United States and part of the same population concentration, is mapped with less than one-tenth of that road density is because of the vast areas of the North which have no improved roads at all. Southern Canada has a very fine road system. Much of the United States is served by a sparse distribution of its roads, particularly in the western half of the country. There are 3.5 million miles of mapped road in the United States and about two-thirds of them are surfaced. The road system is a part of the settlement, serving residential communities with elaborate roads and highway networks which merge into the street patterns of towns and urban communities. Agricultural regions, ranches, and other forms of settlement have road systems which serve their needs.

While parts of western Europe have a road density matching that of the United States, eastern Europe is far below that standard. The Soviet Union is even lower in road mileage, with something of the same problems as Canada. The vast territory in the northern latitudes and in the cold and dry portions of Soviet Asia are often mapped with no roads at all. China is remarkable for its low mileage of improved roads where, despite the great population, the entire country averages less than one-tenth of a road mile for each square mile of territory. This lack emphasizes the problem of exchanging goods and supplies within the different regions of the country and of serving local needs of each region.

Mileage of roads and highways is restricted in low latitudes, whether they be humid or dry. The great deserts have few roads, and they are those which connect nodes of settlement within the region and which also provide links with outside communities. The humid tropical regions have much the same low density, with roads often leading to coastal cities, to waterways, or to the railroads which enter the territory. In both instances, the restrictive physical and climatic conditions often make road building expensive and difficult.

The building of a road and highway network is a part of the developmental program for each country as it increases its economic stature, develops its set of resources, and provides an improvement in the occupational structure of its settlement. Roads become an accompaniment of progress among developing countries. The road system is changing function in newly developed countries as well as in the older economic regions. Motor trucks and semi-trailers have become larger and more efficient carriers now, and they complement and replace railroads as prime movers of freight on a less costly roadbed. The number of automobiles increases annually in all parts of the world as well as in Anglo-America and Europe where they have been an integral part of the road transportation system for two generations.

The road and highway system is certain to grow as a basic pattern of transportation. Its flexibility is one strong consideration since it can provide routes for the movement of heavy goods into and away from most regions. It is easier to replace the caravan routes of Inner Asia with all-weather roads than with railroads. Roads can carry heavier freight loads than air transports. They can connect interior locations with harbors which can then accept for long trips by ocean shipping vast quantities of the hinterland's production. Roads can carry the goods inland by return trip, too, to aid in the development of the integrated pattern of transport.

The Railroad Pattern

The world's railroad network is less than a century and a quarter old. It was built mostly within the last decades of the nineteenth century and had much mileage added during the first two decades of the present century. Rail mileage reached its peak in the United States during the 1920's and had almost the same history in western Europe. Railroad building in other continents continued after that time so that, even in the 1960's, added railroad mileage has been a part of the program of developing countries. Railroads have been the system of transportation which could move great tonnages of goods, either raw materials or manufactures, and distribute them wherever they were needed within the settled community. Also, they have extended the hinterland from ocean ports so that regions far inland have efficient access to world trade routes.

In 1928 Mark Jefferson, the same geographer quoted previously as he wrote about "The world's city folks," analyzed the world's railway system just at the time that medium of transportation reached its peak importance. His study was timed for a period before the patterns of road and highway systems, of oil and gas pipelines, and of air transportation had become very highly developed. When Jefferson wrote his treatise, water transportation was well established on rivers, canals, lakes, and oceans. At that time, passenger travel for long distances was mostly a part of the railroads' traffic. Automobiles and buses were not yet doing their share of the work. Airlines were new.

Jefferson's study was entitled, appropriately, "The Civilizing Rails."[7] Railroads could haul goods of great volume and weight and could distribute them to the parts of the settlement wherever the rail net extended. Ideas went with the goods, and relationships among people

---

[7]Mark Jefferson, "The Civilizing Rails," *Economic Geography*, Vol. 4, No. 3 (July, 1928), pp. 217-31.

improved by the intercommunication. Also, he observed, "Mobility transforms and ennobles peoples. It has always been so."[8] His study included a set of maps of each continent's railroad network. Each rail line was traced over by a pen which scribed a 20-mile wide zone, ten miles of area on each side of the railroad, for every railroad. Within such strips, Jefferson reasoned, all settlers could obtain their foodstuffs, fuels, building materials, and manufactures by use of the railway. Farming areas could ship their farm products, livestock, and produce. The railroads could haul minerals or lumber. There was a world market in reach of the rails and an invitation to travel far beyond the limits of the local community.

The railroad system described by Jefferson was the first extensive mechanized transportational network ever built on land. The 20-mile strips coalesced over much of North America and Europe, showing that these regions were especially well served. Other continents were shown with networks extending generally from coastal cities inland and forming a modified network for the more extended area of the principal settlement. The 1920 rail patterns were not as extensive as they are today.

A contemporary study of the world railroad lines is shown in this chapter in Figure 5.3. There is nearly the same basic pattern to the rail systems as forty years ago but with important additions in other than the North Atlantic-facing communities. Japan has all of its area well served. The Indian Sub-Continent has added much rail mileage, a holdover from the long-time British influence there. It has the best service of any world area other than the Atlantic region. However, its railroads belong to several different rail gauges making train service less adequate than the general map signifies.

The railroad systems are less well developed in other regions than those just described. Soviet Union has a good network west of the Urals in what has traditionally been designated as European Russia. The pattern is sparse in the far north as it is in most of northern Siberia. East of the Urals the triangular area of the network narrows to become the main lines of the Trans-Siberian and the Turk-Siberian systems, with only small areas of industrialized communities having additional rail mileage. China's dearth of a railroad network is noteworthy. However, recent years have brought the completion of major lines which join with the rail systems of Soviet Union in Asia's interior. Settlements in Australia and New Zealand, in south and eastern Africa, and in south and eastern South America are all served by railroad networks which are oriented to coastal areas. The railroads are part of the areas

---

[8]*Ibid.*, p. 217. (Used by permission of the publisher.)

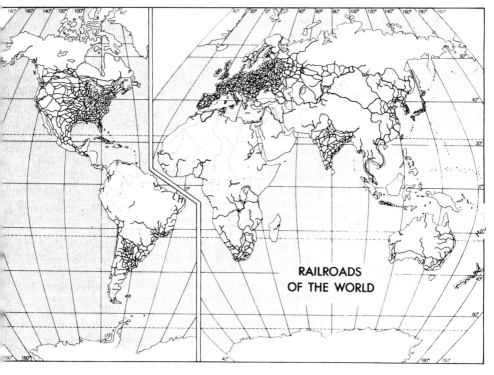

FIGURE 5.3. Railroads of the World
Source: Joseph Bixby Hoyt, *Man and the Earth,* 2nd ed., © 1967, p. 27. Reprinted by permission of Prentice-Hall, Inc., Englewood Cliffs, New Jersey.

of European settlement. The world map shows many other short rail lines, some in interior locations. They often are links in water transportation routes; they lead around waterfalls; or they may be located according to an international boundary agreement.

Railroads still serve as a prime mover of freight, even though in the developed countries generally the passenger traffic has been taken over by other transportation media. Some new railroads are being built to serve specific areas. For example, several recently built rail lines are in operation bringing ores to harbors where ships and barges can take over the longer and cheaper trip to smelters. Railroads are bulk carriers on land now, more completely than ever before. Railroad tonnages are greater now than when the service was more diversified, when passenger, express, and general package freight made up more of the schedule.

Ocean Trade Routes

Ocean trade routes are as significant in the world's transportational system as are the land based patterns. They connect world regions with each other, they touch continental areas at seaport locations where land routes have converged to meet them, and they are the world traffic lines along which move the greatest tonnages of cargoes that travel for long distances in interregional trade. They are a record of the seaports as well, showing where shipping originates and where it is received. This is in turn an evidence of the productivity of the hinterlands of major ports, which are contributing their raw materials or manufactures, as the case may be, to world trade channels.

A map of ocean trade routes and seaports is a record of international trade. Figure 5.4 is a map which shows by the weight of lines the amount of shipping tonnage originating in each port area and the traffic along the shipping lanes. There are three most important features in the world's trade pattern: first, the predominance of the North Atlantic Ocean route as the major path for ocean commerce; second, the network of shipping lines originates at world ports and connects them with other coastal locations, meanwhile encircling continents or converging on ship canals which shorten their length; and third, the world's greatest commercial cities are shown as warehouses for bulk cargoes that make up the world's sea traffic.

Ocean shipping transports bulk cargoes in amounts that dwarf the tonnages carried by any other transportation medium. Shipping varies from small tramp steamers which carry cargo of all sorts along any of the shipping lanes to the mighty bulk carriers which specialize in carrying great tonnages of goods of every kind. They may haul iron ore, iron and steel scrap, bauxite, or coal; bulk cargoes of grain or soybeans; refrigerated and air conditioned consignments of meat, fruits, or bananas; or mixed cargoes of manufactures of every sort from glassware to textiles to automobiles. Of growing importance, especially during the two most recent decades, is the unbelievably large tonnage of the oil-tanker traffic. Such ships are continually becoming larger so that a single tanker load now can keep a refinery at the terminal busy for a long time.

Ocean shipping is a part of the integrated world transportational system. Its role changes with the changes in regional development and with the development of land and air transportation. The shipping lines in the Pacific Ocean carry an increasing amount of tonnage now as compared with the traffic of even a few years ago. The North Atlantic is still the center of convergence for the sea traffic and the region from which shipments of the cargoes of manufactured goods originate. The Panama Canal is very much in demand as a shortener of routes to and from the Orient by the Atlantic communities. Suez Canal becomes less important, seemingly, as oil tankers become efficient so they

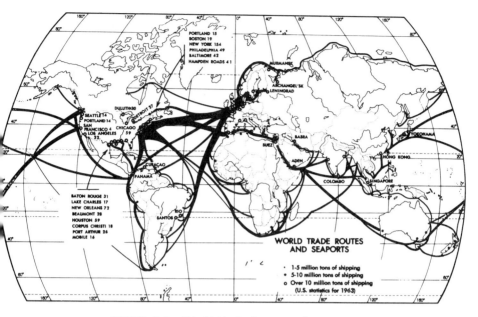

FIGURE 5.4. World Trade Routes and Seaports

Source: Joseph Bixby Hoyt, *Man and the Earth*, 2nd ed., © 1967, p. 406. Reprinted by permission of Prentice-Hall, Inc., Englewood Cliffs, New Jersey.

can encircle Africa on the way from the Persian Gulf to western Europe. This has come about partially because of the current Arab-Israeli crisis.[9]

Ocean trade is international. It aids in the exchange of goods and commodities among regions, items which cannot be locally produced. A great deal of passenger traffic is carried by ships, too, some of it by specially built ocean liners. Like the rail passenger traffic, however, this service is in a decline as air passage becomes more the practice of the traveler.

Other Transportation Media

Many other forms of transportation supplement and complement the three media just described. They must help with the transportation of bulky products, either raw materials or manufactures; and they must make the distributional function flexible enough so that the whole pattern of the community can be serviced. People must be transported, too, as they share in the occupational structure of metropolitan communities or other forms of population distributions. It is impossible even

---

[9]As of this writing, the Suez Canal is still closed to ocean shipping as a result of the Six Days' War in 1967.

to name all these media of transport, because they are ever changing within the areas they serve. A study of these systems, like the major transportation media already reviewed, shows an extreme contrast among developed, developing, and underdeveloped regions.

Metropolitan areas need many forms of transport to move their workers and visitors within their communities. They must have, also, a means of distributing the thousands of items which are needed if the city is to carry on its life and have people served with food, clothing, tools, and all equipment they must have. Subways, suburban trains, elevated electric trains, tunnels, scheduled bus services, and taxis—all are part of the list of transportation media. Heliports add a third dimension to the localized metropolitan traffic.

Air transport of every kind participates in the movement of people and goods in an ever-increasing proportion. It is the newest of the great transportation media, and it is making astounding strides in adding services which compete with the other forms of transportation. Passenger and mail service, air express, and even air cargo take on increasing importance. Planes and air routes can treat land and water the same. They can change routes, change schedules, and adapt to new arrangements among regions, some of them resulting from international bargaining and exchanges. Airlines can connect communities of any size and in any location with any others, in developing as well as in developed areas. They can give efficient passenger service and can carry mail and even light freight to airports in settings which are almost inaccessible by any other medium of transport.

Non-ocean shipments of bulk cargo moves in great tonnages on inland waterways, and on lakes such as the Great Lakes of North America. Barge canals, intercoastal waterways, "inner passages" such as the coast of British Columbia carry a great deal of the transportational load. Giant pipelines carry more oil and gas daily over long distances than a dozen railway trains could carry by a shuttle schedule. All these media are synchronized with the major coordinated transportational network. Electrical transmission lines are almost a form of transportation, as the energy is sent to an area and divided and subdivided so it can be utilized to serve individual needs. These may range from power enough for a jeweler's lathe to the energy needed for a power shovel in a strip mine which can load a railway gondola with one bite.

Communication Systems in Settlement

Communication systems are built into the structure of human settlement, affording the means of coordinating the efforts of the peoples of the world community. Communication media are the nervous system, the means by which a structured social organization can be made functional. They supplement and help the transportational network to serve its purpose, to enable people to live and work in cooperation with each other, and to share local experiences and local products with neighbors near and far. Communication systems are as varied in their forms as transportational forms. They are part of and dependent upon their own regions. They are as varied in kind as coded drum signals are different from satellite-relayed television messages. They have every degree of sophistication possible among both developed and developing countries. In general, major differences among communication systems of different communities are in the proportion of the population which is able to use them. Almost every region named has equipment to transmit or receive exchanges, but few countries have enough equipment to go around for most of the people.

Many kinds of communication systems are built into the landscape. They range from telegraph lines along the railroad to radio and television broadcasting facilities. They may be underground cables or light beacons. Even electric power transmission lines are in between tranportation and communication, since the transmitted energy is the equivalent of fossil fuel that would move by rail, truck, or pipeline. The widespread use of the telephone during this generation of enlarged business connections is an ubiquitous form of communication. Not only spoken messages can be so transmitted, but printed materials such as balance sheets or sketches and diagrams can be transmitted, thus saving time in many ways.

News media are a part of the communication system, whether newspapers, radio, or television. They contribute to intra-regional understanding and to knowing of the events in localities far distant. It is impossible to assess the real value of these media to the creation of world understanding or to realize the responsibilities that result from the ever-widening dissemination of information through mass communication methods.

The responsibilities of the world's communication systems for creating better organized economic systems within world areas are greater than may presently be realized. There is a difference in the use of an integrated system which has within it many forms of communication (telephone, teletype, closed or open circuit television, live news coverage, and dozens of others) with people used to them and dependent upon them for daily briefings, when compared with piecemeal units in use among people with little experience in depending upon them. Underdeveloped countries have too few people available to take advantage of the communication system that much of the world uses. They are handicapped almost beyond repair. The educational opportunities available within developed countries, but unfortunately lagging badly in some developing areas, are related to the degree of acceptance of the communicational network which organizes and integrates the greater social structure of settlement.

Basic Structure of Human Settlement

Human settlement has two components in its distribution. First, there is the physical distribution of population itself, as evinced in the pattern of housing which shows where people live and in what arrangements. Second, there is a set of features also arranged in distributions which indicate the livelihood of an area or region. In the first instance, one can note and record how people are deployed: densely or thinly, nucleated or dispersed. In the other instance, one can observe the occupational structure of the parts of the settlement. Observation can be made as to where men live, how well they live, and what they do to earn their living. Features which show the livelihood structure can be graphically recorded.

The settlement includes rural and urban components. As has been reviewed, the forms of organization differ in both instances from place to place. Also, they vary markedly in different areas according to the interrelated role the urban and rural portions of the settlement play with each other. A significant difference frequently is found among developed and developing countries. In the former, livelihood of the rural area is more closely meshed with that of the region's cities. Employment of rural workers is much like that of their urban neighbors. Rural areas in developing regions are more nearly self-sufficient and self-employing for their own people.

Rural residents of a developed region have a higher proportion of their employment in secondary and tertiary activities than those of newer and less well organized communities. In developed regions, rural districts often are considered residential areas for their cities, i.e., "bedroom communities" for urban employees. Developing countries often have heavy employment in primary industries, producing the first stage of their products for the agents who are to ship the goods to another region (perhaps to a foreign market) or to a manufacturing center within a developed country. Also, there may be in the developing country itself a growing industrial complex which is establishing a beginning of a new stage of occupance.

Transportation and communication continue to play a most significant role in the structure of human settlement. They integrate the whole complex and help give the separate elements a unity of direction and purpose. People and products both must be transported efficiently, economically, and dependably. The communication media must coordinate the total effort. Every form of communication, postal services, telephones, teletypes, radio, and television, aid in organizing a region's or a community's program. Obviously, in less well-developed areas, there are physical handicaps which keep them from competing or cooperating with larger and more remote markets which are suppliers of necessities.

Human settlement is a complex of people earning their living. They have different forms to their occupance, differing with people, with their experiences, and with the resources which they may or may not use within their own physical settings. The local setting may sometimes be restrictive and sometimes helpful to the local community. Activities are built into greater than the local areal relationship. Settlement is within the landscape, and its features are part of the landscape. Thousands of individual features represent what people do and show part of the way people earn their livelihood.

Chapter 6

The Pattern of
Human Settlement

The pattern of human settlement is a complex distribution of man's cultural forms distributed over the earth's surface. He has added his own created features to the natural landscape, sometimes supplanting and concealing the natural features, sometimes avoiding areas which are difficult for him to use in his present stages of cultural development, and sometimes blending his form of livelihood with the natural setting. Population is arranged so that its support can be found in the space it occupies or by some arrangement so that resources of other regions can be brought in to serve the needs of a community which has a special function.

Local support for a settled area can be provided by a quota of arable land and its production or by the advantage of some other resource which can be exchanged with other settled communities. Not everywhere is the state of development at all adequate to provide a suitable living for a region's peoples. There are many seriously underdeveloped areas as observed in Figure 4.1. Even in the case of foodstuffs, there are many regions where now the population depends upon imports, although potentially they could be producers of surpluses of foods which they now import or of other foods of comparable quality in greatly increased amounts. The pattern of settlement shows the same range in development of other than food resources. Minerals, for example, could be produced economically in many regions where there is now only a limited amount of mining activity. Lumbering is another extractive activity which has a highly varied form of development, contributing either much or very little to the livelihood of many forested regions.

There must be a basic food supply for each area of human settlement. Traditionally it has been the practice to consult the tables which show the proportion of arable land available by continent and for the whole of the world's land area. In 1945, an estimate made by Pearson and Harper[1] showed only seven percent of the world's acreage suitable for agriculture. Europe had by far the best rating, with 37 percent; North America had 10.4 percent; Asia had 5.8 percent; Africa with 3.3 percent; and Oceania with 2.9 percent ranked lowest of all. South America, with much of its area in the low latitudes, had a figure showing 4.8 percent of its land suitable for agriculture.

Studies made recently continue to revise upward the proportion of land which can be utilized for crop production. New uses are being found for land formerly considered untillable, as new developments have been made to alter the land itself. More important, however, are improvements which have been made in the crops grown and in tillage practices. Animals and fowls for meat can be produced more efficiently because of new developments in animal husbandry. United Nations teams everywhere are working to raise the level of food production, cooperating with governmental agencies and all levels of community efforts. Many other agencies, such as the Peace Corps, are engaged in the same programs.

Researchers have been at work creating new foods. Synthesis of palatable foods by industrial chemistry is now possible. Former waste foods and non-foods can be converted to staples of human diet. Hundreds of projects are working to derive food from the sea, adding even more to the available food supply for residents on the land. Significantly, despite all efforts, there is a lag in getting food provided for the world's hungry millions and in getting it distributed to where there is need.

Besides the foodstuffs, there is a corresponding inequality in the utilization of other resources. There is still a serious spread between developed and underdeveloped countries. The best forests and the best mineral deposits have been exploited first. In underdeveloped regions, the use of these resources frequently did the residents of those communities very little lasting good. The future is somewhat brighter with more workers participating in the new processes of production, such as mining, ore beneficiation, smelting, and refining. Besides the changes in ore production and processing, there has been developed a long line of substitutions of metals to replace others that formerly were regarded as indispensible. For example, aluminum and magnesium have taken over for some uses of iron and steel. Plastics have often been sub-

---

[1]W. S. Woytinsky and E. S. Woytinsky, *World Population and Production,* Twentieth Century Fund, New York, 1953, p. 50. (Used by permission of the publisher.)
These authors quoted a table by Frank Pearson and Floyd A. Harper, *The World's Hunger,* (Ithaca, N. Y.: Cornell University Press, 1945), p. 50.

stituted for metals of every kind, and they may even be more efficient in filling needs than are the costlier metals they are replacing.

Man is able to create new tools and to invent new processes and new ways of doing everyday things. This is true whether he is offering a more sophisticated device to a primitive social group to replace a bird snare or whether he is arranging data so an elaborate electronic computer can help him find answers for the location and building of an hydroelectric dam in a remote district. Much of his effort creates further inequalities at first among developing nations. A part of the program of the future is to coordinate the efforts for a better living in all parts of the world settlement.

As has been noted repeatedly in this study, the world has presently many more than three billion inhabitants. These people must all live on and be supported by the world's land areas. Without Antarctica, there are about 52,180,000 square miles of land surface, constituting about 29 percent of the total surface of the earth. Enough people are living at this date to make about 57-60 inhabitants for each square mile of land. That figure broken down further means that each person has for his share a square tract hardly larger than one-eighth mile on each side. That length is often noted as a "long-block" in the survey of a city, where frequently there can be counted eight blocks to a mile.

The space available to each human resident is frighteningly small, whether averages are considered or not. Of course, there is no way of finding an average tract which would fill in the picture of one's individual heritage. However, the reader may recall that only seven percent of the parcel is arable. It must produce basic foodstuffs. This tract must include the individual's share of the world's wastelands: mountains, deserts, glaciers, brackish swamps, or stony pavements. It has mines, forests, rivers, shorelines, and harbors. It has homesteads, factories, and cities. It has roads, pavements, parking lots, railroads, airports, and broadcasting stations. Altogether there must be on each person's share of the earth's surface all parts of the settlement structure or there must be arrangements to trade and exchange the production of this territory with others so the functional structure of it all can be maintained. The differences again appear when considering the role of the developed, the developing, and the underdeveloped communities.

Human population is growing at a faster rate than ever before in history, as shown in earlier chapters of this study, especially in Chapter 2. Many countries will have their population double within the lifetime of their adult peoples, TABLE 2.6. Health measures of all sorts, medicinal advances, better diets, and better measures of distributing foods to needy areas have added longevity and a net population increase in most of the world's regions. The responsibility for giving better living to all of the population is far from won. Problems are not clearly understood, and solutions cannot easily be found. This generation is struggling with the questions of a universal program of birth control and population growth restriction. Many instances are found where the expanded resource base is not keeping up with provision of a minimal living standard for the expanding population.

Enough has been learned in the drive to help even the most needy areas of settlement gain a better living to show that better communications and exchanges among regions are necessary. Human ecology is different from that of animal or plant life. Man has the ability to change and alter his environment. He can adapt himself to new sets of conditions because he can anticipate and understand them and in some degree can altar them to serve his own ends. He can increase the quota of arable land, and he can continue to develop a cultural pattern which will utilize newer materials to serve human needs. He can change his form of occupance so that he uses new ways of supporting larger and yet larger numbers of people.

The pattern of human settlement in the future must become more extended than presently, with a population made to cover more and more of the land, with a denser population pattern (*Frontispiece*). Population densities will increase everywhere. Significantly, the highest intensive growth will occur first in the regions which now have major population concentrations. The stage of occupance of such regions, providing an organized industrial structure and good transportation and communication with other areas, will encourage their growth. Developing regions will gain ground as they create for themselves better cultural and economic structures. Fuller use will be made of marginal areas than presently in developing and developed countries alike. Already this has begun with countries assessing their physical resources and beginning to make better use of their potentials. Human settlement is extending areally and economically and culturally. It is not a uniform growth nor a growth which will bring enough assistance for all the earth's inhabitants to soon give them a better living. Population will continue to increase, and accompanying that growth will be redoubled effort to provide the resources for living.

Bibliography

Alexander, John W. *Economic Geography*. Englewood Cliffs, N. J.: Prentice-Hall, Inc., 1964.

Dicken, Samuel N. and Pitts, Forrest R. *Introduction to Human Geography*. Waltham, Mass.: Blaisdell Publishing Company, 1963.

Espenshade, Edward B., Jr. (ed.). *Goode's World Atlas*, 12th edition. Chicago: Rand McNally & Company, 1964.

Hoffman, Lawrence A. *Economic Geography*. New York: The Ronald Press Company, 1965.

Hoyt, Joseph Bixby. *Man and the Earth*, 2nd edition. Englewood Cliffs, N. J.: Prentice-Hall, Inc., 1967.

Jefferson, Mark. "The Civilizing Rails," *Economic Geography*, Vol. 4, No. 3 (July, 1928), pp. 217-31.

—————. "Distribution of the World's City Folks," *Geographical Review*, Vol. 21, No. 3 (July, 1931), pp. 446-65.

—————. "Great Cities of 1930 in the United States with a Comparison of New York and London," *Geographical Review*, Vol. 23, No. 1 (January, 1933), pp. 90-100.

Odell, Clarence B. (ed.). *The World, Its Geography in Maps*, 2nd edition. Chicago: Denoyer-Geppert Company, 1967.

Petersen, William. *Population*. New York: The Macmillan Company, 1961.

Population Reference Bureau, Inc. *Population Bulletin*, Volumes 16 (1960) through 24 (1968), especially. Washington, D. C.

—————. "World Population Data Sheet," for 1968 and earlier issues.

Reuter, Edward B. *Population Problems*, 2nd edition. New York: J. B. Lippincott Company, 1937.

Spencer, J. E. and Thomas, William L. *Cultural Geography*. New York: John Wiley & Sons, Inc., 1969.

Thoman, Richard S. *The Geography of Economic Activity*, 1st edition. New York: McGraw-Hill Book Company, 1962.

Thrower, Norman J. W. (ed.). *Man's Domain: A Thematic Atlas of the World*. New York: McGraw-Hill Book Company, 1968.

Trewartha, Glenn T., Robinson, Arthur H., and Hammond, Edwin H. *Elements of Geography*, 5th edition. New York: McGraw-Hill Book Company, 1967.

United Nations. *Demographic Yearbook,* Series 1955 to 1967. New York: United Nations, 1955 to 1968.

Woytinski, W. S. and Woytinski, E. S. *World Population and Production, Trends and Outlook.* New York: Twentieth Century Fund, 1953.

Index